ACHIEVE

FIND OUT WHO YOU ARE, WHAT YOU REALLY WANT, AND HOW TO MAKE IT HAPPEN

Dr. Chris Friesen, Ph.D.

Bulk Purchases, Speaking, & Consulting

For information on discounts for bulk purchases, to invite Dr. Friesen to speak at your next event, or to work one-on-one with Dr. Friesen, visit FriesenPerformance.com or send an email to Info@FriesenPerformance.com

ACHIEVE

Find Out Who You Are,
What You Really Want,
And How To Make It Happen

- Are you unsure of your life's purpose?

- Are you afraid you're living below your true potential?

- Do you have trouble staying motivated and focused on your goals?

If you answered yes to any of the above, this book is for you.

Dr. Friesen pulls from his work with high achievers, his own personal experiences, and his vast knowledge and experience in the field of psychology to build you a roadmap to elite achievement.

This scientifically packed and highly practical book is going to show you, step-by-step, what you need to do to make sure you're working effectively toward the dreams and goals that are right for you. Whether you're an elite athlete, entrepreneur, executive, professional, writer, or high achiever of any type, this book is for you.

ACHIEVE will help you:

- Learn how your unique personality is the foundation for your success.

- Quickly find out what's really important to you.

- Unleash unique strengths and passions that will be key to your success.

- Unveil the mission and purpose that will propel you forward.

- Learn how to set, and finally achieve, the right goals for you.

Are you ready to take your life to the next level? If so, let's do this!

Dr. Chris Friesen, Ph.D. has always been fascinated by what makes people successful. He helps professional, national/Olympic, and up-and-coming elite athletes, as well as other high achievers such as professionals, entrepreneurs, executives, academics, and writers, achieve their personal and professional potential. He is currently director of Friesen Sport & Performance Psychology. To follow him or to find out more, visit FriesenPerformance.com.

YOUR FREE GIFT

Thank you for choosing *ACHIEVE: Find Out Who You Are, What You Really Want, And How To Make It Happen.* As a thank you for your interest in this book, I'm offering a free bonus infographic on *What Differentiates Truly Successful People from the Rest* and the *ACHIEVE* Framework. Head to <u>FriesenPerformance.com/Achieve-Free-Gift</u> to download it now!

CONTENTS

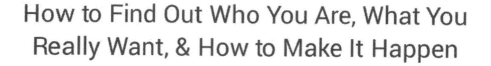

How to Find Out Who You Are, What You Really Want, & How to Make It Happen

Know Your
PERSONALITY

Make it Happen
EVERY DAY!

Identify Your
VALUES

ACHIEVE

Set
GOALS

Discover Your
STRENGTHS

Choose Your
MISSION &
PURPOSE

Introduction

WHAT'S IN THIS FOR YOU?

I'm just going to put it out there — I bet, like most people, you're performing below your potential. If you're like me, you probably have goals and aspirations you would do almost anything to achieve. I believe in having no regrets and leaving no stone unturned.

Imagine this: Your goal is to make your country's Olympic team. This is your dream. You're getting "old" and this is the last year you'll be able to compete. You wake up on the day of the Olympic trials and look at yourself in the mirror. Do you want to be able to honestly say to yourself that you've done everything in your power to get yourself ready for this moment?

Your response to this question will predict whether you are or aren't going to perform to your full potential.

Or maybe your dream is to get into the top medical school or take your start-up business to the next level. Whatever the dream, the principles are the same. You only get one shot at this life, so make the best of it. No regrets.

Before we go any further, I want to ask you some serious questions. Take a moment to answer these as honestly as possible. Have you:

- Felt different from others, but were not quite sure why?

- Felt unsure of your purpose in this life?

- Wondered whether you were focusing on the right goals in your life?

- Felt certain paths you took, or decisions you made, just didn't seem to fit?

- Wondered whether your chosen career path was right for you?

- Felt you were just going through the motions in your life?

- Had trouble staying motivated and focused on a big goal?

- Established your big goals, but couldn't seem to stay motivated long enough to make them a reality?

- Felt unsure of yourself and in your ability to accomplish your goals?

Most people say yes to many of the questions above. If you said yes to any of them, you're reading the right book at the right time. My goal is to help you find some answers.

This book is going to show you, step-by-step, what you need to do to make sure you are working effectively toward the dreams and goals that are right for you. We'll cover the WHY, WHAT, and HOW of setting and achieving the right goals.

Many books assume you know what you want and get right to what you need to do. This book spends a lot of time on helping you really get to know yourself first. This is essential if you want to make sure you focus on the right things. It's a mistake to focus on goals without doing the hard work of really getting to know who and what you are.

The key to success is to **know your *WHY* — your purpose or mission**. And to really find out what your purpose or mission is, you need to know your core personality and what you truly value. Only then can you try to discover how you can use your strengths, interests, passions, talents, and skills to work toward your purpose or mission.

Once you know your purpose and mission, then you can choose goals that truly are meaningful to you and then work toward them. This book ends with detailed strategies to make sure you can stick with your goals on a day-to-day basis. This entire process is the key to your ultimate success and happiness.

HOW THIS BOOK SERIES IS DIFFERENT

This is the first book in The High Achievement Handbook series. Through publishing this series, my aim is to ensure that you're doing the right things to live up to your true potential.

In today's day and age, we seem to have less time than ever before. There is an unbelievable amount of useful knowledge coming out of the fields of psychology, physiology, neuroscience, and others. It's not easy to sift through it all and figure out what's useful and what isn't. My goal is to do this for you. I want to break through the clutter and confusion and bring clarity to what you should be doing in order to reach your potential. For those of you willing to harness this knowledge, the sky is the limit.

So what will this book do? Using what I believe are the three best sources of knowledge — science, personal experience, and results — it will give you *what* you need to know, *why* you need to know it, and *how* to start doing it and reap the benefits of reaching your potential. It will do so in a series of straightforward and logical steps.

First and foremost, the steps and strategies in this book series are based on scientific research. There are a lot of books and programs out there filled with things that have no scientific backing or have actually been shown to be ineffective when tested.

One example is positive affirmations. Telling yourself you're awesome or that you'll be successful is a staple of many self-help books. Recent research by Dr. Joanne Wood[1] has shown that, while repeating positive affirmations may be mildly beneficial for people who already have high self-esteem, it has the opposite effect for those whose self-esteem is not so high. When those with lower self-esteem practiced positive self-statements, their moods actually worsened. On the other hand, when those with low self-esteem were allowed to think negative thoughts, their moods improved!

Second, the steps and strategies in this book series were chosen because I currently use them or have used them myself in the past. It's one thing for me to read about something in a scientific journal or in a self-help book, but quite another to try it out on myself. I personally need to not only see something to believe it, I also have to experience it myself to *truly* believe it.

Last, I've only included steps and strategies that I've seen work on others in my own clinical work and in my consulting with high achievers.

While this book will lay out the path to achieving great things with your life, the path is not necessarily easy or simple. Too many self-help books or online magazines try to make things so easy with titles like "5 Simple Steps to Achieve Any Goal Without Breaking a Sweat!" If it were that simple and easy, you wouldn't be reading this book. So if you're tired of the quick-fixes and ready to do the work to finally take your game and life to the next level, you're in the right place.

WHO IS THIS GUY?

So who am I to give you advice on how to reach your potential? Good question. Like you, I'm just a guy who wanted to reach his potential and do something he loved to do. I have no special talents or intellectual superpowers. What I have done is taken what I've learned so far in my life personally, as a psychologist, and from what has helped others and applied it to myself and my clients. I've learned to harness the power of my personality, values, interests, strengths, and weaknesses. By doing this, I have figured out my current purpose and mission in life. I then applied what I

---

[1] Dr. Joanne Wood's study: http://pss.sagepub.com/content/20/7/860.abstract

learned about setting and achieving goals in my life. I will share these strategies with you in this book.

I'm definitely not perfect and must continue to work to reach my full potential. That's a lifelong quest that never ends — a process, not an outcome. At the same time, because science and experience are constantly evolving, I know even better strategies and techniques will emerge in the future. This book series describes the best of what we know today.

Like many, I struggled with low self-esteem and anxiety, especially in my early teens. As a teen, I also underperformed in school. My grades were terrible. I'll never forget the day in eighth grade when I was one of two students forced to tour the basic-level high school primarily reserved for delinquents. This was one of the roughest schools in the city, with gang fights and rampant drug dealing. I clearly remember the sheer terror I felt on the tour of that school.

This incident served as my own Scared Straight experience and motivated me to pull up my marks for the last semester, ultimately allowing me to enter the same high school as my friends. And thank goodness for that! In the process of writing this book, I unearthed a number of news stories from the time when I would have attended that school detailing gang attacks, stabbings, and even the shooting of the school guidance counselor and assistant principal by a student. (Thankfully, they survived!). The school was closed at the end of that year.

Don't get me wrong, I wasn't a delinquent. It was just that my grades were terrible, and that was the school you went to when you were getting grades in the 50s and 60s. Although this motivated me to do what I had to do to get by, it didn't unleash the motivation to perform at my highest potential. This, of course, makes sense to me now. I had only half the motivation equation covered — fear. What I didn't have covered was a real passionate reason to do my best in school. So my grades continued to flounder until my final year of high school.

During my early teens, my passion was instead fueled by playing hockey as a goaltender. I started playing at age 12, which by Canadian standards is late in life. Despite struggling academically and having problems with low self-esteem and anxiety, especially in academic contexts, I found both my comfort and passion in hockey. I started to build what psychologists call self-efficacy — a belief in my ability to accomplish something. I had a very low sense of self-efficacy before hockey entered my life. I soon realized that, if I put my mind to it, I could excel in hockey.

I started to read self-help books like Tony Robbins' *Awaken the Giant Within and Unlimited Power*[2]. I also read what may well be the best self-help book ever written, Stephen Covey's *The 7 Habits of Highly Effective People*[3]. These books were major eye-openers for me. I had no idea how much control I could have in my life if I really put my mind to it and I've been fascinated by human potential ever since.

And it started paying off. Suddenly, I went from being the worst goalie in the local house league to the best. The next year, I made the all-star team. The year after that, I skipped a skill level and earned a position on the team that had won the league championship the year before. The more I applied my passion and discipline and what I was learning from self-help books, the more I improved.

Still, in reality, I remained on the verge of flunking out of school. I was much more interested in sports than reading Shakespeare. I finally made the top level in hockey for my age group and I would have been eligible to be drafted into the Canadian Hockey League. But I was cut from the team after playing only one game. My new team's former goalie had been cut from the CHL and my new team wanted him back. At this level, it was all about winning, so my new team let me go.

This was a painful experience for a 16-year-old kid, but it quickly hit me. If I didn't take control of my life, life was going to take control of me. I came to the painful realization that a career as a professional hockey player was not in the cards for me.

---

[2] Awaken the Giant Within and Unlimited Power by Tony Robbins http://goo.gl/lJw02A and http://goo.gl/9yelC4
[3] The 7 Habits of Highly Effective People by Stephen Covey: http://goo.gl/g79501

I also realized how much I loved learning and reading about psychology, exercise physiology, nutrition, and self-help, and passing along what I learned to anyone who would listen. I realized I wanted a career related to this passion, and so it was time for me to do something about this.

I figured I might be able to take what I had learned from sports and self-help books and apply it to my studies, despite my original lack of belief in my abilities as a student. Amazingly, it worked out enough to get me accepted into university so I could achieve my goal of a career that kept me interested and fulfilled. It wasn't long before I realized that, if I worked hard enough and focused on what interested me, I could get good grades in university.

At the time, this was a complete turnaround for me. In fact, in high school, I had such a low opinion of my academic potential that my dad had to practically write my term papers for me! Of course, once I moved away from home to university, getting help from my dad was no longer an option. This was in the pre-Internet era! Amazingly, as I found my passion for learning about the body, health, and psychology, I surprised everyone around me, including myself. I got even better grades on my university papers than I did on the high school papers my dad (who is a great writer, by the way) practically wrote for me! This blew me away.

It was at this point in my life that it really hit me. I realized I could do almost anything I put my mind to, if I wanted it badly enough. Combining my interests, love of learning, drive to improve, and the lessons and strategies I learned through sports, psychology, and self-help books, I completed two undergraduate degrees and won an award for the highest GPA of all psychology majors. I was eventually accepted into a graduate clinical psychology program. My friends and family were just as surprised as I was by this reversal.

This course of events taught me to never underestimate myself or others. We all have much more potential than we believe. This is not to say that I breezed through life after that point. But through the challenges I faced, I learned that things that seem scary or impossible have to be faced head-on. I also learned that it's OK to have self-doubts, as long as we use them to keep us humble and help us move toward our goals and values. These lessons propelled me through my master's and Ph.D. degree programs. They also propelled me through my various clinical internships, residency, and post-doctoral clinical training.

I knew I wanted to study and work with others who, like me, wanted to maximize their potential. But I also knew that to fully understand people, I had to work with people of all types.

Despite self-doubt and fear of the unknown, I repeatedly sought to work with the most challenging patient populations. Through my training and work as a licensed clinical, forensic, and neuropsychologist, I assessed and treated a broad spectrum of people, including those with anxiety, depression, personality disorders, dementias like Alzheimer's disease, brain injuries (from sports concussion to severe traumatic brain injuries), and problems with the law (offenders of all types).

To be able to help people reach their potential, I believed I needed to thoroughly understand and help people of all types, including those who were at their lowest points and those who were not living up to their potential.

This long process of graduate school and clinical training pulled me away from my original goal of studying and working with those who wanted to take their lives to the highest level. It took some time, and the implementation of many of the strategies outlined in this book, to get me back on track toward helping athletes and other individuals performing at the highest levels continuously improve and achieve their potential.

After a combination of 13 years of clinical training and university study, I eventually came full circle. I now work with high achievers of various types. Many of my clients are elite athletes, whether they be professionals, Olympians, or up-and-coming athletes with significant potential.

I also work with other high achievers such as professionals, entrepreneurs, executives, academics, and writers. To help illustrate some of the power of the techniques and strategies that I will teach you in this book series, I will use many of my clients as examples, with their identities and certain facts changed to preserve their anonymity.

The fact that you are reading this book means we likely have a lot in common. We have the drive to take our game and lives to the next level. We want to make sure we're focused on the right strategies and techniques and are not wasting our time. If this is you, then you're in the right place.

I want to re-emphasize something I know I keep repeating. One thing I've learned from my own personal experience, my studies, and my work with others is that we often have much more potential than we or others believe. We also have much more control over our life trajectories than we appreciate. The first step in reaching your potential is to know yourself, your personality, values, strengths, weaknesses, and passions! Without this knowledge, you will never reach your true potential.

We need to know what turns us on and what turns us off. We need to know our personalities, our strengths, and our weaknesses. We need to figure out what we truly value in life and establish our long-term goals. Then we must work hard. Let's not kid ourselves. You don't achieve big goals by sitting around dreaming about them, or by just thinking positive thoughts. Glory doesn't come from easy victories. It comes from achieving ambitious goals that were difficult to attain.

Think about which scenario will lead to a sweeter victory:

1. Having to barely train or face a significant challenge in order to win an Olympic gold medal.

    OR

2. Working your butt off in training and then going to war against the most challenging competitors the world has to offer and coming out on top.

Or what about this:

1. Making partner at your firm after six months on the job due to your good looks, who your previous employer was, or who your father was.

   OR

2. Starting from the bottom, working your tail off for three years, and then making partner based on your blood, sweat, and tears.

You know the answer.

When I first came up with the idea of writing this book series, I wanted some form of a written manual or handbook for my high-achieving clients. I then realized such information might have wider appeal. And I thought I might be able to improve on some of the books out there.

I've read hundreds of psychology and self-help books. Some of these I love (e.g., Covey's *7 Habits of Highly Effective People*). Others, not so much.

I wanted to write a book that had the elements I liked — e.g., action steps — without the ones I didn't like — 300+ pages, endless description of research studies, few real-world examples, and a lack of information about the author's experience with the methods they were recommending.

THE PROMISE OF THIS BOOK

Of course, this book is not about me; it's about you. So you may be asking, what the heck am I going to get out of reading this book series? My goal is to provide you with a series of go-to manuals on the exact steps you can take to help bring you one step closer to unleashing your potential. I want you to leverage the science of sport/performance psychology, executive coaching, and cognitive neuroscience to maximize both your personal and professional potential.

What I don't want to do is bore you with endless details. My goal is to give you just enough information so you understand the What and Why behind each strategy so you can start using them to change your life for the better.

Each of the strategies I will outline has scientific backing. I've also used them in my own life. You see, I know how powerful scientific research is, and I use this as my starting point. As I mentioned earlier, for me to truly believe in a strategy, technique or hack, I have to try it out on myself first before I can really buy into it.

Most importantly, I use them with my high-achieving clients, whether they be professional athletes, students, or entrepreneurs. When science, my experience, and my high-achieving clients get great results, then I add the strategies to my toolkit. The strategies in this book and others in this series have not only turned my life around —they've changed the lives of the high achievers I've worked with.

I promise that, if you implement only a few of these steps and strategies, your performance will improve and you will be that much closer to reaching your goals. If you implement most of the steps and strategies, you will drastically improve your performance beyond what you may have thought was your potential. You can rest assured that you are doing exactly what you need to be doing to ensure your success.

So the question becomes: Do you want to live with regrets because you didn't do all you could to achieve your dreams and goals, or do you want to be able to look yourself in the mirror each day and feel confident that you are doing everything in your power to reach your goals?

If your answer is the latter, then you're in the right place. The strategies and techniques you are about to learn will take your game to the next level. You are about to learn how to unleash your potential and find out who you are, what you really want, and how to make it happen. I want to say congratulations for taking this first step.

Are you ready to take your life to the next level? If so, let's do this!

BONUS MATERIAL:

Visit friesenperformance.com/achieve-free-gift to download the ACHIEVE Framework.

STEP 1

KNOW YOURSELF

Chapter 1

TAKING STOCK OF WHO YOU ARE

The journey of a thousand miles begins with one step.
— Lao Tzu

*Permanence, perseverance and persistence in spite of all obstacles,
discouragements, and impossibilities: It is this, that in all things
distinguishes the strong soul from the weak.*
— Thomas Carlyle

Britain's Danny Williams is no ordinary boxer. Unless you're a hard-core boxing fan, you've probably never heard of him. Although he fought and beat an "old" Mike Tyson in 2005 and even challenged reigning WBC champ Vitali Klitschko, that's not why I'm bringing him up. What is remarkable about Williams is his heart.

This was remarkably displayed early in his 20-year boxing career when he faced off against another Brit named Mark Potter in 2000. To call this fight dramatic would be an understatement. By all accounts, the fight was supposed to be fairly even. But in Round 1 Williams was knocked down by Potter. Then in the 3rd round, Williams suffered one of the most painful and dreaded injuries when his right shoulder dislocated. He couldn't move his arm.

Most mere mortals would have called the fight and given up, assuming we had an almost zero chance of winning a match that required above all else the use of our arms.

At the end of the third round, one of Williams' cornermen tried to push his shoulder back into its socket. Seeing this, the fight's promoter, Frank Warren, begged Williams to stop the fight. To the shock of the packed crowd in the Wembley Conference Centre, he refused.

Amazingly, with only one arm properly functioning, Williams fought through the next two rounds, even though Potter tried to take advantage by repeatedly punching Williams' damaged arm and shoulder. The referee did nothing.

As the sixth round began, Williams looked like he was recovering somewhat. He was able to bend his arm in an attempt to protect his chin from Potter's relentless attacks. But this lasted only about 15 seconds before his shoulder dislocated once again.

Everyone knew it was only a matter of time before either the referee stopped the fight or Williams succumbed to Potter's blows. But the crowd couldn't help but feel a sense of awe at what they were witnessing. How was this guy doing it? How could he withstand the pain? Didn't he know he was finished? Why didn't the bloody ref stop the fight?

"They have to call the fight!" the color commentator kept repeating. "He's going to get knocked out! ... He's in a no-win situation!"

Despite the pain and the odds, Williams was not about to give up his Commonwealth title or cede the vacant British title. No way. He had trained too hard and too long for this. He believed in himself even when nobody else did. He normally fought orthodox — or right-handed — he kept fighting just like he always had, but now only using his left arm.

What happened next is the stuff of legends. Even Stallone couldn't have written a more dramatic ending. Williams kept pushing forward, catching Potter with a perfect left uppercut that sent him to the canvas semi-conscious.

Potter rose to his feet before the 10-second limit. Williams attacked again with his one and only weapon — his left arm. He swung once and missed. He swung again — and connected! Potter staggered, and fell to one knee. He again made it to his feet before the limit, but the momentum was no longer in his favor. Once the referee signaled the fighters to engage once more, Williams charged Potter again with nothing but his one arm and his unbreakable spirit.

Williams connected, and Potter crumpled. The referee was having no more of it. Against all the odds, Williams triumphed! The color commentator could barely comprehend what he had witnessed. Even Britain's own ultimate tough guy chef and star of Hell's Kitchen, Gordon Ramsey, can be seen ringside standing and staring in disbelief.

After the fight, Williams said simply: "I would never quit!"

What is it that Williams tapped into to keep moving forward despite the pain and odds? Was he stupid? No. Does he have something most of us lack? No.

He showed heart and an unstoppable spirit because he had an overarching goal, a mission, a purpose that was bigger than the pain. Bigger than the fear of getting knocked out. Bigger than the fear of permanent injury.

In battling the odds to become the British and Commonwealth Heavyweight Champion, Williams demonstrated a number of the primary differentiators between those of us who are successful in sport, business, and life, and those of us who aren't. These differentiators are learnable. So what are they?

THE SEEDS OF SUCCESS

Successful people know themselves well; they grasp their strengths and weaknesses and then live their lives based on their deepest values, mission, purpose, and goals, and not based on their immediate urges, moods, or circumstances. Nietzsche said it best, "He who has a why to live can bear almost any how."

Successful people know that they have much more control over the trajectory of their lives than most people realize. They know and accept that they will repeatedly go through rough waters. They know that's how the world works and don't fight or complain about it. They also know that if they keep pushing forward, they will eventually reach their destination.

They also know that even though they are steering their ship, they can only control what has been given to them. They accept themselves for who they are and work with or around what they are given. They know they can't control what the world throws in their path, but they can control how they react to this. They know that they can anticipate and act before the world acts upon them.

They also know that once they get to their destination, there will be another destination they would like to visit on the other side of the horizon and that the cycle will continue. Because of this, they accept and enjoy the struggle, as they know that the journey *is* the destination.

So what does this mean for you? This means that you need to accept and live your life like successful people. So you should:

- Know and accept your strengths and weaknesses, and work with or around what you are given.

- Live your life based on your deepest values, mission, purpose, and goals, and not based on your immediate urges, moods, or circumstances.

- Realize you have more potential than you already believe.

- Realize that you have much more control over the trajectory of your life than you already believe.

- Accept that you will repeatedly go through difficulties. Don't fight or complain about it. Instead learn and grow from it.

- Know that you can anticipate and act before the world acts upon you.

- Know that if you keep pushing forward, you can eventually reach your destination.

- Know that you can't control what the world throws at you, but you can control how you react to this.

- Know that once you achieve your goal, there will be another goal you will want to achieve.

- Know that the journey *is* the destination. Accept and enjoy the struggle and triumphs.

- Realize that whatever path you choose, it's going to be hard and painful at times. You need to be ready for this and accept it as worthwhile if you are to live the life you really want.

KNOW YOUR DESTINATION

If I'm to help you become truly successful, we need to make sure you know yourself and where you really want to go. In other words, you need to know your WHAT and your WHY. There's nothing worse than relentlessly pursuing a goal, and then coming to realize it was not the right goal for you. This has become all too apparent with many high achievers I've worked with.

I once worked with a young and highly talented basketball player named Leroy. Leroy rocketed up the ranks and was playing for one of the top college basketball teams. But his performance was progressively worsening. At first, everyone thought he was struggling to adjust to the faster pace of college play and the combination of academic, social, and athletic demands placed on college basketball players. But when his performance continued to slide in his second season, his coach insisted he see a sport psychologist.

After we worked together for a few weeks, it became apparent that Leroy struggled even to motivate himself to apply the strategies we discussed in the sessions. He admitted he hated being in the spotlight and all of the buzz around basketball. He told me that he often felt annoyed and overwhelmed by all the noise and chatter in the locker room and on the court. He didn't feel anxious; he felt overstimulated, which is common for those who share his basic personality tendency, which I will discuss later in this book.

Leroy told me that, ever since he was a young kid, he was taller than his peers and basketball came easily to him. As a teenager, people started to give him more respect and attention because of his basketball talents. Prior to this, he felt that nobody thought much of him or his future. Suddenly, his family started to talk about how he was the one child that would "make it." Like any kid, he was encouraged by this attention to continue to pursue basketball.

But through our discussions, I noticed he never spoke about having a strong passion for the game. Instead, he talked about feeling obligated to his family, friends, and coaches to not let them down. He noticed how his family would often joke about the expensive things that he could buy them once he made it to the NBA. This also served to motivate him to continue with basketball.

As we got to know each other, I asked him about his passion for the game. He gave me flat responses. I asked him if his dream was to play in the NBA. Surprisingly, Leroy said that nobody had ever asked him that, and that he was unsure. I asked what he would do with his life, if money were no object. He was unsure.

Leroy was studying criminology at university because he always had been fascinated by detective stories and crime shows. He admitted that, even when he was a young teenager, he often read books in bed when nobody was around, as reading was not something his family or siblings valued. Surprisingly, he never paid much attention to basketball or other sports on TV.

But his coaches and even his professors seemed to expect him to put little energy or effort into his studies. The message he was receiving was that he was there to play basketball and that academics were of little importance.

Leroy lit up when describing his favorite detective novels and crime shows and all the ways detectives could find their suspect with a mixture of old-fashioned detective work and modern forensic technology. He also lit up when talking about his criminology courses. When he talked about this interest with me, it was like I was talking to a completely different person.

Although it took some time, Leroy finally admitted to himself that he almost hated basketball and was really only playing to please others. He eventually admitted he felt trapped and dreaded a future in basketball. Of course, he admitted that making a lot of money in the NBA would be nice, but he really didn't believe he could put in the work it would take to make it. He realized that basketball was taking away from his chance to achieve his real dream, which was to become an FBI agent.

After lengthy and heartfelt discussions, it became very clear that Leroy never really loved basketball and his lack of passion for the game was not something I could help him with. Without this passion, it is extremely difficult to make it to the top. The only thing I could do was help him figure out what he really wanted to do with his life. Leroy ultimately gained a better understanding of his personality, values, strengths, and interests using a number of the strategies outlined in this book.

In the end, Leroy decided to finish his second basketball season while doing his best not to let his studies slide. He wanted to make sure he would have no regrets if he stopped playing. In the end, he did stop playing. He sends me occasional updates and last I heard he still has no regrets.

After he stopped playing, his grades skyrocketed and he was a changed person. He went from being a kid living out the dreams of others to a man living out his own. He was accepted into one of the country's top master's degree programs in criminology and couldn't be happier. He found a calling that was in line with his personality, values, and natural interests.

There is nothing worse than going through years of blood, sweat, and tears pursuing a goal that ends up being the wrong goal for you. Leroy is one of the lucky ones. There are many worse stories of athletes and others who pursued the wrong goals for the wrong reasons, and, as a result, ended up being miserable. Often they don't even know why. Sometimes they become depressed, anxious, and addicted to substances to get by.

Don't let yourself be one of them. Following the steps and doing the exercises in this book will help ensure you are on the right path for you.

Chapter 2

KNOW YOUR CORE PERSONALITY TENDENCIES

The most difficult thing in life is to know yourself.
— Thales

You can't drive a car until you know how it works. Or at least, you can't drive it *well!*

The same is true when it comes to your life. Without a solid understanding of your basic temperamental personality traits, what I call your Basic Personality Tendencies, you will find yourself frustrated and ineffective trying to live up to your potential. So in this chapter, you're going to learn about your core personality.

One of the biggest mistakes most self-help books make is to assume we are all the same. I believe the one-size-fits-all strategy is one of the primary reasons most self-help books don't lead to any lasting change for the majority of people reading them. Also, many self-help books are written by people with no training or serious study of human nature. Without this training, they often are unable to critically evaluate scientific research to determine whether their advice has any merit.

On the other hand, when books on psychological topics are written by academics, they often are laden with science, but weak when it comes to translating that information into actionable strategies that people can actually use. Conversely, there is a huge body of research on personality that has not made it into public consciousness.

That's a shame because psychologists from around the world have produced consistent findings in the measurement of our basic temperaments or personality traits. This subject has been near and dear to me for a long time. In fact, my undergraduate and master's theses dealt with what kinds of things our personalities predict, from adjustment and success in university to political orientations. My Ph.D. dissertation was also about how our personalities predict the types of psychological problems we develop.

That said, there are a number of personality measures being sold to people and businesses that are not based on good science. These measures are primarily sold and used by people with little to no training in psychology or personality, such as business consultants, executive coaches, and life coaches. If you've ever taken any of these assessments, don't put a lot of weight on the results. If you plan on taking one, or if someone like an executive or life coach tries to convince you to take it, tell them you'll pass.

Many of these measures like to pigeonhole people into personality "types." The idea that you neatly fall into one of a number of supposed personality "types" is flawed and not well supported by research. Personality psychologists have found that categorizing people into types is not a very accurate way to describe personality. We are much more nuanced than that; people just don't fall into neat little boxes.

Any serious personality researcher measures traits on a continuum or spectrum, not as an either-or proposition. Cross-cultural personality research has found that we all tend to differ across five to six global personality dimensions, each made up of a number of different but related traits that will be discussed below. Many popular measures sold to businesses are missing some of these key personality dimensions.

For example, one of the most obvious ways we differ from one another is in our tendency to experience negative thoughts and feelings. I refer to this as Negative Emotions — short for Susceptibility to Negative Emotions and Stress. This dimension is not even measured by some of the most popular measures used in business and by life and executive coaches.

The nail in the coffin for many of these personality "type" measures is that they have been shown to be unreliable. When a measure is unreliable, it is by definition invalid. In other words, useless.

For example, independent researchers have repeatedly administered these personality "type" measures multiple times to large groups of people only a few weeks apart. They found that a large portion obtained a totally different result or "type" each time they took the test. By definition, personality traits are enduring ways of acting, thinking, and behaving. Personality is not the same as your current mood and doesn't change week-to-week. So if you get a different result each time you take the test, then it can't be a valid measure of personality.

So don't make any decisions or draw any conclusions about yourself after taking any of these popular personality "type" measures. No serious personality psychologist uses them anymore, as there are much better measures available that are in line with modern personality research which don't have such fatal flaws.

WHAT YOU CAN AND CANNOT CHANGE

One thing you need to know and accept is that there is a continuum of what you can and cannot change about yourself. Some things, like height, are essentially unchangeable once you become an adult. Other things like muscle composition are alterable to a certain degree, depending on a number of factors, including your genetics. The same thing goes for your psychological makeup.

Your Basic Personality Tendencies are difficult, but not impossible, to change at the core. Your tendencies are essentially hard-wired into you starting from a young age due to a combination of the genes inherited from your family and your various experiences.

The neural pathways in your brain that control these are repeatedly activated on a daily, if not minute-to-minute basis for years and years. The repetitive activation of your basic personality strengthens these neural pathways, making them harder and harder to change the older you get.

Although much of your Basic Personality Tendencies are difficult to permanently change, things like values, beliefs, attitudes, interests, goals, habits, and self-perceptions are much more malleable. Before we get to some of your more easily modifiable features, though, first we must help you learn about your Basic Personality Tendencies.

Living your life or pursuing goals that are incongruent with your Basic Personality Tendencies invites failure. In a ground-breaking book, *Personality in Adulthood*, the National Institute of Aging's personality psychologists, Robert McCrae and Paul Costa, found that our personalities are set like plaster by the time we reach the age of about 30. They and other personality researchers from around the world have repeatedly found that, despite what happens to us (e.g., divorces, job losses, lottery winnings, deaths of loved ones), our Basic Personality Tendencies don't change much over our lifespans.

This may sound depressing to some, but let me clear up what I mean and don't mean by Basic Personality Tendencies:

- Basic Personality Tendencies do not refer to our beliefs, values, interests, talents, or IQs.

- Basic personality refers to temperaments that are present at birth, then shaped by life experiences. About 40 percent to 60 percent of our basic personality is considered heritable. This means they are inherited from our parents in our genes or the result of "nature." The rest is considered to be influenced by "nurture" — what we experience in life.

Anyone with multiple children will tell you that each child came into the world with their own unique personalities, despite few changes in parenting styles, nutrition, and home environments between siblings. So make no mistake — Basic Personality Tendencies are real and have a huge impact on our lives.

MINDSETS

I want to make something clear at this point. I'm not suggesting that our personalities are unchangeable. There is accumulating evidence of something called neuroplasticity, which refers to the fact that we can change our brain functioning through changes in lifestyles, daily habits, and through other experiences.

But this can only go so far when it comes to Basic Personality Tendencies. It is very rare to take someone who is extremely outgoing by nature and turn them into someone who is introverted for more than a short period of time. And that's not really the point, anyway.

Changing basic personality should not be the goal for most people. The goal should be to come to know their Basic Personality Tendencies and learn to either work around them or work with them along the path to success. That said, some may need to change their personality as much as they can in a direction that is more conducive to reaching goals that are in line with their values and purpose.

And there is hope for those who want to work on a Basic Personality Tendency. There is a significant body of research that suggests that if you believe that your personal qualities and abilities can change — if you have what Stanford psychologist Carol Dweck calls a "growth mindset" — then you are more likely to be able to change them. On the other hand, if you believe your traits and abilities are fixed, you are unlikely to be able to change them. With a growth mindset, you are more likely to challenge yourself and persevere in the face of setbacks.

So let's assume that you are in the early stages of getting your start-up off the ground and you believe you are an anxious introvert. You know that eventually you're going to have to pitch to investors to secure the needed funding for your product. If you have a fixed mindset, you're going to have a hard time believing you can pitch and schmooze with investors. You'll either avoid doing this or try to pawn it off on someone else. You'll probably say to yourself: "I'm way too anxious and reserved to pitch and mingle... I'm just not like that."

But if you took on a growth mindset you would realize that even as a temperamentally anxious introvert, you could improve by working on your anxiety, presentation skills, and ability to charm and engage in small-talk. The growth mindset would enable you to alter your behavior, at least temporarily, or even possibly change your personality to a certain extent.

In the majority of people, personality traits are relatively enduring ways of thinking, feeling, and acting, but this does not mean that personality tendencies are unchangeable. If you believe they are unchangeable, they will be. If you believe there is leeway, you will be able to adapt your personality somewhat to suit your values and purpose.

Stanford psychologist Carol Dweck and others have now measured the effects of mindsets, but the wisdom has been known for much longer: Confucius said: "He who says he can and he who says he can't are both usually right."[4]

Resources

Carol Dweck, Ph.D. who is the primary researcher in the area of growth vs. fixed mindsets. Check out her book Mindset here: http://goo.gl/IB9tYD

- Personality In Adulthood: A Five-Factor Perspective (2nd Edition) by Robert McCrae, Ph.D., & Paul Costa, Ph.D.: http://goo.gl/RURCXw

---

[4] Confucius quote: https://goo.gl/q4VHkl or: http://goo.gl/0gvZaK

The Owner's Manual For Personality At Work: How the Big Five Personality Traits Affect Performance, Communication, Teamwork, Leadership, and Sales by Pierce Howard, Ph.D., & Jane Howard, M.B.A.: http://goo.gl/9ZO12N

Chapter 3

THE 5 BASIC
PERSONALITY TENDENCIES

*Man's main task in life is to give birth to himself, to become what he
potentially is. The most important product of his effort is his own
personality.*

— Erich Fromm

*Personality is that pattern of characteristic thoughts, feelings, and
behaviours that distinguishes one person from another and that persists
over time and situation.*

— E. Jerry Phares

For more than 70 years, personality psychologists have sought to determine just how many basic personality tendencies or dimensions there are. Approximately 55 years ago, sophisticated statistical techniques narrowed down the thousands of ways we can describe personality into 5 global personality dimensions. Since that time, researchers have repeatedly reconfirmed this discovery and there is now general agreement that there are essentially 5 global dimensions of personality across cultures.

In this book, I will discuss the 5 Basic Personality Tendencies, each of which is made up of numerous related sub-traits. Also, each of these personality dimensions is distinct. In other words, your standing on one dimension is unrelated to your standing on any of the others. Below are the 5 Basic Personality Tendencies, with a bold label showing how I will refer to them throughout this book:

- **Negative Emotions:** Susceptibility to negative emotions & stress

- **Extraversion:** Tolerance for external stimulation

- **Openness:** Degree of openness to change & new experiences

- **Agreeableness:** Attitude toward others

- **Motivation:** Degree of motivation & self-control

WHERE DO YOU FALL ON THE 5 TENDENCIES?

I'd like you to rate yourself on the following 5 Basic Personality Tendencies. Try to reflect on how you have generally thought, felt, and behaved over the past few years. The goal is to get a measure of your personality, not your current state of mind. If you feel unsure, ask a few people who know you well where they would rate you. This is only meant to give you a general idea as to where you likely fall and is not a diagnostic test.

Bear in mind that not every descriptor within each of the 5 Basic Personality Tendencies will describe you well. They are provided to give you a general idea of what sub-traits tend to make up the overall dimension. Read all the descriptors and then decide where you think you fall on each Basic Personality Tendency. Keep in mind, there are no "good" or "bad" profiles.

Put a check mark in one, and only one, of the six boxes for each of the 5 Basic Personality Tendency descriptions:

Susceptibility to Negative Emotions & Stress

I tend to be:

Extremely High ☐   Very High ☐   High ☐

- Worried, anxious, nervous, or tense a lot

- Easily stressed

- Annoyed and irritable often

- Discontent or moody

- Pessimistic

- Easily panicked when stressed

- Often motivated by fear and the threat of losing something (e.g., money, health, relationships)

OR

I tend to be:

Low ☐   Very Low ☐   Extremely Low ☐

- Rarely worried

- Calm almost all the time

- Patient and even-tempered

- Content

- Rarely stressed by difficult situations

Extraversion/External Stimulation Tolerance

I tend to be:

Extremely High ☐   Very High ☐   High ☐

- Extraverted/outgoing/social
- More interested in doing things with people than alone
- High energy
- Attracted to excitement/stimulation from people or situations
- Easy and quick to feel positive emotions
- Enthusiastic

OR

I tend to be:

Low ☐   Very Low ☐   Extremely Low ☐

- Detached
- Reserved and serious
- Most comfortable and interested in working alone
- Even paced
- Avoidant of too much excitement/stimulation from people or situations
- Slow to experience and show lots of positive emotions
- Less enthusiastic

Openness to Change/New Experiences

I tend to be:

Extremely High ☐ Very High ☐ High ☐

- Creative

- Artistic or very interested in the arts

- Imaginative

- Curious and interested in new and diverse subjects or people

- Highly attuned to and valuing emotions and gut feelings

- Willing to experiment and try new and exotic things

- Intrigued by and open to different points of view

OR

I tend to be:

Low ☐ Very Low ☐ Extremely Low ☐

- Down-to-earth

- Practical

- More interested in logic than gut feelings and emotions

- Focused on a narrower or more predictable range of interests

- Traditional

- Conservative in my perspectives

- Clear with what I believe is right and wrong

Agreeableness

I tend to be:

Extremely High ☐   Very High ☐   High ☐

- Quite trusting
- Open and revealing with my thoughts and feelings
- Highly concerned with helping others
- More interested in cooperation over competition
- Lenient towards others' shortcomings
- Deferring to others
- Modest
- Highly sympathetic and easily moved by others' pleas

  OR

I tend to be:

Low ☐   Very Low ☐   Extremely Low ☐

- More skeptical and not easily duped
- Guarded with what I share with others
- Focused on my problems and goals
- Self-protective
- Competitive
- Vocal about what I disagree with
- Proud and not afraid to let others know
- Tough-minded and objective

Motivation/Self-Control

I tend to be:

Extremely High ☐   Very High ☐   High ☐

- Self-controlled
- Disciplined
- Competent
- Goal-oriented
- Ambitious and driven
- Detail oriented
- Organized and planful
- Efficient
- Deliberate (take a lot of time to make decisions)

OR

I tend to be:

Low ☐   Very Low ☐   Extremely Low ☐

- Unsure of my abilities
- Inefficient
- Turned off by schedules
- Disorganized
- Undisciplined
- Low in ambition and drive
- Avoidant of big and ambitious goals
- Very spontaneous (make decisions without too much thought)

**These descriptions are primarily based on the work of Costa & McCrae[5].

Take note of how you or close others rated you on each of the 5 Basic Personality Tendencies because your knowledge of this is key to your success. These traits are your strengths and weaknesses.

A current fad in self-help books, stemming from a misunderstanding of the work in the field of positive psychology, emphasizes that we should focus on our strengths and essentially ignore our weaknesses. This is a reaction to psychiatry and clinical psychology's strong focus on what's wrong with people. I agree that we should be focusing on our strengths, but we need to know our weaknesses and either work around them, with them, or on them, depending on our goals, values, and purpose.

Each Tendency is a Potential Tool

Each of the 5 Basic Personality Tendencies can be a strength or a weakness depending on the circumstance. Each is evenly distributed throughout the population with most of us falling near the middle of the extremes. This even distribution makes sense from an evolutionary perspective. Having members high and low on all 5 tendencies played an important role in our survival as a species when we lived in close-knit communities or tribes.

For example, having a subset of the population that is highly motivated, efficient, and ambitious is essential to a tribe's ability to do the work that needs to be done to survive and thrive.

Perhaps less obvious is the value of having a certain segment of the tribe that is highly susceptible to negative emotions, thoughts, and stress. The reality is that these individuals were highly valuable for their ability to perceive and respond to environmental warnings associated with some form of threat, such as changes in weather patterns or threats from other tribes

---

[5] See Robert McCrae, Ph.D., & Paul Costa, Ph.D. *Personality in Adulthood: A Five-Factor Perspective* (2nd Edition): http://goo.gl/XjCtLQ

and animals. So having members who were high or low on each of the tendencies was adaptive for the tribe's survival and ability to flourish.

This is important as we continue our discussion of understanding yourself. It will also help you understand which areas outlined in this series of books you will likely need to work hardest on to make sure you are performing to your potential.

Now that you know where you stand on each of the 5 Basic Personality Tendencies, it's time to figure out what that means in terms of finding out who you are, what you really want, and how to make it happen.

BONUS MATERIAL

Visit FriesenPerformance.com/Achieve-Bonus-Materials to download additional Basic Personality Tendencies rating sheets.

Chapter 4

SUSCEPTIBILITY TO NEGATIVE EMOTIONS & STRESS

Susceptibility to Negative Emotions & Stress:

I tend to be:

Extremely High ☐   Very High ☐   High ☐

- Worried, anxious, nervous, or tense a lot

- Easily stressed

- Annoyed and irritable often

- Discontent or moody

- Pessimistic

- Easily panicked when stressed

- Often motivated by fear and the threat of losing something (e.g., money, health, relationships)

OR

I tend to be:

Low ☐ Very Low ☐ Extremely Low ☐

- Rarely worried

- Calm almost all the time

- Patient and even-tempered

- Content

- Rarely stressed by difficult situations

On one side of the scale for this Basic Personality Tendency are those of us who are more prone to worry, self-doubt, pessimistic thoughts, and feeling tense, stressed, anxious, moody, or discontent.

On the other end – the "low" end — are people who are calm, patient, content, and rarely affected by stress.

Those in the middle ground on Negative Emotions will likely feel most comfortable with either a balance between stressful and relaxing experiences in life, or with a lifestyle that is at most moderately stressful.

THE NEUROSCIENCE
OF NEGATIVE EMOTIONS

Where you fall in terms of Negative Emotions may be at least partially related to the neurotransmitter serotonin in your brain. Serotonin functions to improve and balance our moods, among other things. You've probably heard of the antidepressant fluoxetine, better known as Prozac. It is a serotonin reuptake inhibitor — or SSRI — which is a fancy way of saying it increases the amount of usable serotonin in the brain. SSRIs have been found to improve mood and reduce most types of negative emotions such as anxiety and anger. Altering the amount of usable serotonin in the brain has been shown to also alter levels of the Basic Personality Tendency of Negative Emotions[6].

Your level of Negative Emotions is not only related to your neurotransmitters; it's also related to how active your limbic and sympathetic nervous systems are. These systems control your fight-or-flight response. This response is activated in all of us when stressed. You know what it feels like when this system is activated. You feel your heart rate increase, muscle tension grow, hands become sweaty and cold, and your breathing quicken. This comes on when you are feeling negative emotions like anxiety or anger.

Those of us who are higher on Negative Emotions have a lower point at which our stress response kicks in when faced with stressors. Consistent with this, newer MRI research has found that your standing on Negative Emotions is related to differences in activity in brain areas that control how sensitive you are to threat and punishment.[7]

If you also are high on the next dimension — Extraversion — then you are probably very emotional. You're apt to experience high levels of both negative and positive emotions which, like all traits, can be helpful in some circumstances and unhelpful in others. You probably live with passion and excitement that others will easily pick up on. As long as you can keep your negative emotions reasonably controlled, your passion will likely be contagious and you may gravitate toward leadership positions, especially of groups with meaningful causes. But if you let your negative emotions reign, you'll be prone to experience life as an emotional roller-coaster. This can wreak havoc on your interpersonal relationships and your ability to achieve your goals.

You may be a bit confused by the fact that your tendency to experience positive emotions is related to Extraversion rather than Negative Emotions.

---

[6] Knutson et al., (1998). Selective alteration of personality and social behavior by serotonergic intervention. The American Journal of Psychiatry, 155(3), 373-379.
[7] DeYoung et al., (2010). Testing predictions from personality neuroscience: Brain structure and the Big Five. Psychological Science, 21(6), 820-828.

Most people believe that positive and negative emotions are at opposite ends of a continuum. It turns out research has repeatedly shown that positive emotions and negative emotions have little relationship when it comes to our personalities or our usual way of feeling, thinking, and behaving.[8] Of course, if you are in the throes of a major depressive episode or anxiety disorder, you are going to have a hard time experiencing positive emotions regardless of where you fall on Extraversion.

Neuroscience research suggests that positive and negative emotions are controlled by different areas and networks within the brain. For example, research has found that having high negative emotions is correlated with over-activity in the brain's right frontal lobe, which is located behind the right side of your forehead. On the other hand, having low levels of positive emotion has been found to be associated with under-activity in the left frontal lobe.[9]

Research has also found that a deep brain structure called the nucleus accumbens is involved in the experience of positive emotions. Negative emotions tend to originate in two almond shaped structures in an area deep within the limbic system of the brain known as the amygdala, which is more reactive in those with higher levels of Negative Emotions.[10]

How long or how intensely negative emotions affect you depends on differences within the left front part of your brain known as the left prefrontal cortex. A "stronger" left prefrontal cortex can inhibit or calm down the amygdala.

Work by neuroscientist Richard Davidson, and others has found that this is related to the amount of connections between the prefrontal cortex

---

[8] Watson, Clark, & Tellegen (1988). Development and validation of brief measures of positive and negative affect: The PANAS scales. Journal of Personality and Social Psychology, 54(6), 1063-1070.

[9] Davidson (1992). Emotion and affective style: Hemispheric substrates. Psychological Science, 3(1), 39-43.

[10] Depue & Collins (1999). Neurobiology of the structure of personality: Dopamine, facilitation of incentive motivation, and extraversion. Behavioral and Brain Sciences, 22, 491–569.

and the amygdala.[11] The good news is that the number of connections between these areas appears to be changeable with training such as mindfulness meditation and possibly through a burgeoning area of training known as neurofeedback. I will be providing more information on these in the upcoming books in this series

HIGH NEGATIVE EMOTIONS

If you are high in this tendency, you will tend to have trouble controlling your negative emotions and thoughts, and become easily stressed and overwhelmed. Negative emotions can include anxiety, self-consciousness, anger, and sadness.

In addition, the higher you are on this dimension, the more likely you are to experience other difficulties, such as inhibiting your impulses to do things that you know you shouldn't do, like overeating, drinking too much alcohol, overspending, and saying things in the heat of the moment that you later regret. You are also more likely to have unrealistic expectations of yourself or others, be pessimistic, feel self-conscious, worry too much, and avoid risks and other things that make you uncomfortable.

The Basic Personality Tendency of Negative Emotions is so powerful that, when not controlled, it is the underlying cause of most anxiety and depressive disorders. It can also underlie many addictions. It's easy to think of the many famous artists and athletes who turned to drugs and alcohol because they could not tolerate or control their negative thoughts and feelings. I've worked with many athletes who finally made it to the top only to crumble under internal and external pressures due to their inability to tolerate, control, and harness their negative emotions, whether it is anxiety or anger. It's unfortunate that it required a massive failure for them to realize that they should work on their mental game and call me.

---

[11] Davidson (2012). The Emotional Life of Your Brain: How its Unique Patterns Affect The Way You Think, Feel, and Live-and How You Can Change Them. http://goo.gl/PVSDbK

On the other hand, if you are high on this cluster of traits and learn to tolerate, control, and harness your negative emotions, you can use this tendency to your advantage. Many high achievers I've worked with have learned to harness the power of their negative emotions to improve their performance. For example, the simple act of relabeling anxiety before major competitions or performances as feeling "ready to go", "amped", or "pumped" often significantly improves performance. Those high achievers who tolerate, control, and harness their negative emotions and thoughts are often those who become the most successful, because they have a passion that others don't.

Similarly, having high Negative Emotions is a hallmark of successful artists. For example, when creating works of art such as paintings, sculptures, novels, and screenplays, tapping into negative feelings is essential to spark creativity. Most successful novelists and screenwriters capitalize on this ability to help them feel empathy and develop and understand characters. Their passion comes out in their art.

If you fall on the high end of this spectrum, the strategies throughout these books will be of most benefit to you. I will explore ways to manage your susceptibility to negative emotions and stress in much more depth in the upcoming books. For example, if you change your perception of what it means to experience negative emotions so you can view these emotions as a powerful source of energy, you can use it to your advantage. Think of these negative emotions like a wild horse. You can either let it trample and destroy you, or you can learn to tolerate, control, and harness its power.

WHAT IT MEANS FOR YOUR ACHIEVEMENT

There are significant obstacles facing those of you who are high on Negative Emotions and high on the dimension of Motivation/Self-Control. You are at risk for failure when it comes to achieving big and ambitious goals. You'll likely be very intense and focused, but you'll have a hard time controlling your stress response and mood, as well as feelings of inadequacy and anxiety. If so, you'll likely undermine your ability to reach your big goals, unless you harness these tendencies. You will be prone to crumble under the stress and pressure you will face when trying to achieve big things. You'll also be prone to burnout.

The good news is that the tools and strategies laid out in this series of books are tailored for those of you with this profile. The current book helps you learn about who you are, what you value, and where and how to focus your drive. With your natural drive and motivation, the tools and strategies outlined in the last chapter of this book, and especially the information in the upcoming books in this series will provide you with the best chances of reaching your true potential.

For those of you who have high Negative Emotions and low Motivation, the odds of becoming a high achiever or reaching big and ambitious goals are much lower. You at least need motivation and drive. It must be there, whether it comes from a long-standing Basic Personality Tendency, or from developing your mission or purpose through clearly identifying your values, strengths, passions, and goals.

However, if you are high on Negative Emotions and low on Motivation, being a high achiever is not impossible. You'll have to develop a very clear and strong passion, mission, and purpose, and then work very hard implementing the strategies in this series of books to learn to tolerate, control, and harness your negative emotions.

WILL IT BE A STRENGTH OR A WEAKNESS?

High levels of Negative Emotions can be a strength and a weakness, depending on how you handle it. If you can tap into the energy, drive, and passion it provides, it can serve as a strength. If you let it get in the way of living the life you want, it's a weakness.

The key is to know where you stand on this personality dimension, determine what your values, strengths, passions, purpose, and goals are, and then decide where in your life it is helping and where it is hurting. Then learn to accept it, change it, or harness it. Your Negative Emotions threshold can be altered with the strategies covered in the upcoming books in this series, but you must believe it can be changed by having a growth mindset as noted earlier.

Low Negative Emotions

Those of you on the opposite extreme, who have little susceptibility to negative emotions and stress, have a lot more leeway under stress before your emotional brain or limbic and sympathetic flight-or-fight systems are activated. In other words, you are naturally calm under pressure. For the most part, being unshakable is a strength for obvious reasons.

Those with low Negative Emotions tend to do well in professions where keeping emotions in check is really important, even a matter of life or death. For example, it's essential for pilots and surgeons to have few difficulties with negative emotions, since high levels of negative emotions often lead to irrational thinking and poor decisions.

Low Negative Emotions Isn't Always a Good Thing

As with all of the Basic Personality Tendencies, low levels of Negative Emotions can be a potential strength or a liability, depending on the situation.

Having very low levels of Negative Emotions can lead to problems with empathy and indifference to the feelings of others. If you experience few negative emotions, it may be hard for you to understand what it feels like for others to have these feelings, or to predict how your actions may cause negative emotions in others.

Much of our learning, especially as children, comes from our experience of negative emotions when we do things wrong or engage in inappropriate behaviors. If we don't experience much negative emotion, we often don't learn socially appropriate behaviors.

If we have very low levels of Negative Emotions, we can also fail to appreciate our own limitations and vulnerabilities, and fail to perceive the dangers, risks, or consequences of our behavior.

Many elite athletes and other high achievers seek me out in an attempt to eliminate high negative emotions. But having low levels of negative emotions and stress is not necessarily a good thing.

I've worked with numerous athletes in combat sports who say they want to be more like this guy or that gal who appear to have no fears or worries before and during competition. Once I educate them further, they realize it's impossible for them to have no fears or anxieties, and that it's also not in their best interests. The reality is we need a certain level of anxiety or emotional activation to perform at our best.

As discussed above, we need to learn to tolerate, control, and harness our negative emotions, not eliminate them. Also, without fears and self-doubts, we'll have a hard time motivating ourselves to improve. "No fear" can lead to complacency.

WHAT IT MEANS FOR YOUR ACHIEVEMENT

Those of you low on Negative Emotions and high on Motivation have a personality makeup tailor-made for high achievement. You're good at setting goals and working through the inevitable stresses you will have to face when trying to achieve them. You're inclined to have high levels of self-esteem and the ability to cope with setbacks well. Failures are more easily seen as lessons learned, and you are less discouraged by them. You persist until you've overcome any challenges or setbacks.

If you are low on Negative Emotions and high on Extraversion, you tend to be optimistic and confident and simply enjoy life. Other people probably love being around you, given your positivity and high spirits. You may be rarely overwhelmed by problems and highly attuned to the good things in life. You tend not to look back or get stuck in the past, preferring instead to anticipate all the positive possibilities in the future. This optimism and positivity can help ease your path toward high achievement.

If you happen to have a strong tendency to experience positive emotions, a trait associated with Extraversion, you probably feel generally happy most of the time. Research indicates that our well-being or happiness levels tend to be stable across our lives, regardless of what happens to us. The good and bad things that happen to us affect us in the short-term, but don't have much effect on our long-term happiness.[12] [13]

Happiness is primarily related to our standing on Negative Emotions and Extraversion. Where you fall on Extraversion and Negative Emotions will generally determine your "set point" with regard to your sense of well-being and happiness. Of course, this set point is movable to a certain degree, depending on how hard you work. Many of the strategies in this series of books will help you move your set point on Negative Emotions a little lower and your set point on Extraversion a little higher.

Of course, happiness is much more than feeling free of negative emotions and feeling strong positive emotions. To be truly happy, you also need a number of other things. And in my opinion, the happier you are in the broader sense of the word, the more successful you will be in reaching your goals.

There are whole books and psychology labs around the world dedicated to studying happiness. The best model that I have found was developed by Martin Seligman, now considered the "father" of the sub-field of Positive Psychology. There were many before him that got little press, including Abraham Maslow, Carl Rogers, and Rollo May — all part of the humanistic human potential movement that began after World War II and took off in the 1960s. But it was Seligman who brought the study of human potential back to life and attempted to make it more of a scientific pursuit than a philosophical one. Seligman and others have found that what should be considered as happiness is really a combination of a number of factors.[14] These factors make up the acronym P.E.R.M.A. and include the following:

---

[12] Haidt (2006). The Happiness Hypothesis: Finding Modern Truth in Ancient Wisdom. http://goo.gl/IkQ81S

[13] McCrae & Costa (2005). Personality in Adulthood: A Five-Factor Perspective (2nd Edition). http://goo.gl/XjCtLQ

[14] Seligman (2004). Authentic Happiness: Using the New Positive Psychology to Realize Your Potential for Lasting Fulfillment. http://goo.gl/xz1LiM

- **Positive Emotions:** Experiencing and focusing on positive emotions and having a realistic-to-optimistic outlook. This is primarily related to Extraversion.

- **Engagement:** Being engaged in and absorbed by activities. This is often referred to as getting into "flow" or the "zone."

- **Relationships:** Social connections are important to everyone. Your standing on Extraversion and Agreeableness heavily influence your relationships.

- **Meaning:** Living your life with a sense of purpose and meaning. This includes living your life in line with your values and is a major focus of the current book.

- **Accomplishment:** Making and achieving goals, the focus of the last few chapters of this book. This is heavily influenced by your standing on Motivaton/Self-Control.

So you need a high level of engagement in the things you spend your time on in addition to experiencing positive emotions. When you are absorbed in what you're doing, you are fully in the present moment. This can also be referred to as "flow" or being in the "zone."

You also need meaningful relationships. You don't need a ton, but most of us need to have at least some positive and meaningful relationships to be happy and successful. For those of you who are low on Extraversion and low on Agreeableness, getting and maintaining close and meaningful relationships will be somewhat more challenging and will take much more work on your part.

Seligman also notes that true happiness stems from having a sense of meaning or purpose in your life. You need a strong reason or set of reasons for why you do what you do. Otherwise, what's the point?

You also need a sense of accomplishment. Having a sense of ambition and setting and achieving obtainable goals will give you a sense of accomplishment. Just working toward goals tends to increase a person's sense of satisfaction. Once you reach your goals, you will feel proud and fulfilled, at least for a while. People feel most alive when they push themselves to do something bigger.

CONCLUDING THOUGHTS

Those of you who are low on Negative Emotions will have the least need to work on some of the strategies in the upcoming books in this series. However, even if you are low, having a well-rehearsed arsenal of strategies to reduce stress or over-activation will be helpful when you face big challenges such as your debut at the Olympics or your pitch in front of your ideal investors.

Key Takeaways

- The Basic Personality Tendency of Negative Emotions contrasts those more prone to worry, self-doubt, pessimistic thoughts, and feeling tense, stressed, anxious, and moody with those who are calm, patient, content, and rarely affected by stress.

- This dimension is related to the neurotransmitter serotonin and to the activity of the limbic and sympathetic nervous systems that control the fight-or-flight response.

- Because your standing on Negative Emotions can either make or break your success, you need to know where you fall on this dimension and work around or with it.

- If you are high on this dimension, then you need to learn to tolerate, control, and harness your negative emotions if you want to reach your potential.

- The key to success is not having very low levels of negative emotions. Anxiety and self-doubt can help you succeed if you harness what these offer you.

- Your standing on Negative Emotions and Extraversion determines your "set-point" for your sense of well-being and happiness.

- Many of the strategies in this series of books will help you move your Negative Emotions set-point a little lower and your Extraversion set-point a little higher.

- True happiness in the broader sense is related to more than low levels of negative emotions and high levels of positive emotions. It is also related to your level of engagement in your life, the quality of your relationships, your sense of purpose and meaning, and your sense of accomplishment.

Resources

The Happiness Hypothesis: Finding Modern Truth in Ancient Wisdom by Jonathan Haidt, Ph.D.: http://goo.gl/IkQ81S

Authentic Happiness: Using the New Positive Psychology to Realize Your Potential for Lasting Fulfillment by Dr. Martin Seligman, Ph.D.: http://goo.gl/xz1LiM

The How of Happiness: A New Approach to Getting the Life You Want by Sonja Lyubomirsky, Ph.D.: http://goo.gl/bu3C1q

The Emotional Life of Your Brain: How Its Unique Patterns Affect the Way You Think, Feel, and Live--and How You Can Change Them – by Richard J. Davidson, Ph.D.: http://goo.gl/PVSDbK

Chapter 5

EXTRAVERSION/EXTERNAL STIMULATION TOLERANCE

Extraversion/External Stimulation Tolerance

I tend to be:

Extremely High ☐   Very High ☐   High ☐

- Extraverted/outgoing/social
- More interested in doing things with people than alone
- High energy
- Attracted to excitement/stimulation from people or situations
- Easy and quick to feel positive emotions
- Enthusiastic

OR

I tend to be:

Low ☐ Very Low ☐ Extremely Low ☐

- Detached

- Reserved and serious

- Most comfortable and interested in working alone

- Even paced

- Avoidant of too much excitement/stimulation from people or situations

- Slow to experience and show lots of positive emotions

- Less enthusiastic

People high on Extraversion are more interested in doing things with people than alone. They also tend to be outgoing, energetic, attracted to excitement and stimulation, and quick to feel positive emotions intensely.

This contrasts with those low on Extraversion who are more detached, reserved, serious, comfortable and interested in working alone, who avoid too much excitement and stimulation, and are slower to experience and show a lot of positive emotions.

If you are in the middle, then you are more "ambiverted." You tend to feel most at home with controlled doses of excitement and stimulation, mixed with adequate time scheduled for solitude. You probably display some of the strengths and weaknesses associated with high and low levels of Extraversion described in this chapter.

HIGH EXTRAVERSION

THE NEUROSCIENCE BEHIND HIGH EXTRAVERSION

If you are high on Extraversion, then you will need to match your day-to-day environment with your need for external stimulation. This trait has been found to be related to neurotransmitters in the brain such as dopamine. Extraversion appears to be highly related to the brain's reward pathways. For example, multiple MRI studies have found that one's level of Extraversion is positively related to the size of the medial orbitofrontal cortex, a part of the brain that determines how rewarding external stimuli are. Similarly, it's believed that dopamine makes things in your environment appear more attractive and thus more rewarding.[15]

In general, potential rewards in your environment like food, sex, social interactions, money, or other goals trigger the release of dopamine in the brain, which in turn produces positive emotions and attraction to these things. This motivates us to actively work toward obtaining these rewards. This is one reason why Extraversion is related to energy and activity levels. It's theorized that those higher on Extraversion experience stronger positive emotions in response to things in their environment due to a stronger and more frequent activation of the dopamine response.

The cerebral cortex is the outer 2 mm to 3 mm of your brain that controls things like vision, hearing, bodily sensations, and movement, in addition to more complex functions like memory, language, abstraction, creativity, judgment, and attention.

Another, somewhat older and possibly overly simplified way of conceptualizing what it means to be high on Extraversion is to think of your cerebral cortex's level of arousal or activation. You can think of this as analogous to a car engine idling. If you are high on Extraversion, then your brain is naturally revving too low. In other words, your cortex's level of

---

[15] DeYoung et al., (2010). Testing predictions from personality neuroscience: Brain structure and the Big Five. Psychological Science, 21(6), 820-828.

activation is likely low. When a car is revving too low, it's at risk for sputtering out or stalling, so to speak.

While your brain won't stall, low levels of cortical arousal can be experienced as boredom. The remedy for this is to give it a little gas. In other words, you need to seek out external stimulation (social or otherwise) in order for your brain to rev at a normal, comfortable level.

THINK OF HIGH EXTRAVERSION IN TERMS OF NEEDS

Sometimes it's best to think of Extraversion in terms of needs. With a high level of Extraversion, you are going to feel most comfortable and satisfied when you get your high needs for external stimulation met either through your job, sport, hobbies, or family life. You will need to have a regular outlet for socializing, experiencing fast-paced, stimulating and exciting things, or expressing your positivity. If you don't, you will be vulnerable to boredom and low moods.

BENEFITS OF HIGH EXTRAVERSION

If you are high on Extraversion, then you will feel at home in fast-paced, exciting, and social environments. You're probably happy and this can be contagious. You are likely to be popular and perceived by others as more attractive than may objectively be the case, probably because you are positive and social. There is even research to suggest that you may even live longer, especially if you are also high on Motivation.[16] [17]

DRAWBACKS OF HIGH EXTRAVERSION

But there are some things to be careful about if you are high on this dimension. You may have difficulty spending time alone, or be overly focused on the number of your relationships, rather than their quality.

---

[16] Danner et al., (2001). Positive emotions in early life and longevity: Findings from the nun study. Journal of Personality and Social Psychology, 80(5), 804-813.

[17] Friedman et al., (1995). Childhood conscientiousness and longevity: Health behaviors and cause of death. Journal of Personality and Social Psychology, 68(4), 696-703.

Sometimes, when your needs for external stimulation are not met, you may feel the urge to engage in attention-seeking behaviors.

You may also have a difficult time slowing down, and your energy levels may be difficult for your friends and family to tolerate or match. Although you'll feel at home in leadership positions, you may also be at risk of coming across as being too pushy, bossy, or curt, especially if you are low on Agreeableness. You may also be prone to getting reckless with excitement-seeking activities, or being too optimistic and positive.

LOW EXTRAVERSION

WHAT INTROVERSION REALLY MEANS

Those low on Extraversion are often thought of as having high levels of Introversion or are referred to as "Introverts." Technically, this is accurate. However, I want to make clear here that what many books on the market today describe as Introversion and what I and personality researchers are referring to here are only somewhat related.

Many of these books describe "Introverts" as those with a combination of traits such as preferring to be alone, being shy, sensitive, intuitive, introspective, and having a rich and expansive inner life. The reality is most of these traits are actually unrelated. This depiction of Introversion is not supported by scientific research. Many of the traits described are actually a description of traits from a combination of 3 of the 5 Basic Personality Tendencies which are unrelated to each other. The description is of a combination of the traits associated with someone who is low on Extraversion and high on Negative Emotions and Openness to Change/New Experiences. So don't confuse what I and personality researchers are talking about and what you hear pop-psychologists talking about.

THE NEUROSCIENCE BEHIND LOW EXTRAVERSION

If you are low on Extraversion, you likely have a less robust dopamine response in your reward pathways when faced with potential external rewards. As noted earlier, dopamine makes things in your environment appear more attractive and rewarding. So for those of you lower on Extraversion, potential rewards in your environment like food, sex, social interactions, money, or other goals likely don't lead to the same significant release of dopamine as is experienced by those who are high on this dimension. This leads to a more muted emotional response and less attraction to these things.

Using the car engine analogy again, if you are low on Extraversion, you can think of your brain naturally revving high. Older research has found that people like you tend to have a high level of natural cortical arousal.[18] Keep in mind that this is not the same thing as anxiety, although when overstimulated you may in fact feel anxiety. Anxiety is part of Negative Emotions.

If you are low on Extraversion, you rarely feel bored when alone or when doing things that may seem boring to an outside observer, especially someone who is high on Extraversion. If you get too much stimulation from external sources, you're predisposed to feel uncomfortable or overstimulated. Your "engine" easily approaches or exceeds the red line when faced with a lot of external stimulation.

What this means for you is that you'll likely need to be very careful with how much external stimulation you expose yourself to. If your sport or job is highly social, fast-paced, or highly stimulating, you'll likely need much more down time off the court or after work to recover.

BENEFITS OF LOW EXTRAVERSION

Being low on Extraversion can be a significant advantage. If you are low on this dimension, you are less likely to be swayed by external things that many others find rewarding. So you are less likely to feel seduced by the latest trends.

---

[18] Eysenck (1990). Biological dimensions of personality. In L. A. Pervin (Ed.), Handbook of personality: Theory and research, 244-276.

Likewise, you're less likely to fall victim to "shiny object syndrome," or the tendency to feel the need to get the latest gadget or product on the market. You'll also rarely get bored and be comfortable when training, studying, or working in isolation for significant periods of time.

WHEN LOW EXTRAVERSION CAN HOLD YOU BACK

In addition to becoming easily overstimulated, you may be at risk of becoming socially isolated. This can lead to problems such as a lack of social support. In order to achieve big goals, we often need the support of others. We also need others for feedback and encouragement, especially when things are not going as well as we hoped.

At big competitions or in business meetings or other social gatherings, you may be prone to feeling overwhelmed and irritated. As noted earlier, being over-activated due to being low on Extraversion is not the same thing as anxiety. You are more likely to feel annoyed or exhausted than anxious if overstimulated.

If you are low on Extraversion, you also may come across as unenthusiastic or uninterested, because you are more reserved, even-paced, or have a more muted expression of positive emotions. Similarly, you may be more likely to have a pessimistic outlook on things, especially if you're high on Negative Emotions. If you have this personality pattern, you may often feel unprepared and quickly overwhelmed by the pressures of life. Many of the strategies outlined in the forthcoming books in this series will teach you effective ways to combat low levels of positive emotions and overly pessimistic thinking.

If you are low on Extraversion and Negative Emotions, you may not experience high levels of either positive or negative emotions. You're pretty even-keel. When everyone else is getting frazzled by an upcoming deadline or big game, you're likely cool as a cucumber.

If you have the low Extraversion and low Negative Emotions profile, you may still dislike too much external stimulation such as lots of socializing, but you probably don't get too upset about it. You may have a hard time getting pumped-up before big games or important events. Others may perceive you as a little bland or cold. So if you are in a situation where you need to display some passion, like when trying to pitch your new script for a TV series to a potential backer, you'll have to work a lot harder to get psyched up to impress the backer with your passion for the project.

CONCLUDING THOUGHTS

Knowing where you fall in terms of Extraversion is essential for your success. Once you have a clear idea of your values, strengths, passions, and purpose, then you will be better able to decide whether you should learn to accept your natural personality tendency or change it. Like your Negative Emotions threshold, whether you can change your set point will depend on having a growth mindset.

Key Takeaways

- Extraversion contrasts those who are social, energetic, attracted to excitement and stimulation, and quick to feel positive emotions with those who are more reserved, comfortable and interested in working alone, and less turned-on by excitement and stimulation.

- Where you fall on the Extraversion dimension is related to your brain's ability to handle external stimulation before getting overwhelmed. Those of you who are high on this dimension enjoy and can tolerate high levels of external stimulation. Those of you who are low will function best with measured doses of stimulation followed by recovery periods.

- Your standing on this dimension is also related to how easily your brain is attracted to, and turned on by external rewards. Those high on this dimension will be easily attracted to and rewarded by things in their environment. Those low on this dimension will be less affected by external rewards.

- You can think of Extraversion in terms of needs. If you are high, then you'll have a strong need for socializing, experiencing fast-paced, stimulating and exciting things, or expressing your positivity. If you don't, you will be vulnerable to boredom and low moods. If you are low, then you will have a strong need for times when you are alone or in relatively quiet environments or you run the risk of feeling overwhelmed and burning out.

- Both high and low levels of Extraversion can be helpful and unhelpful when it comes to success. Knowing the benefits and pitfalls of your specific personality is key to your success.

Chapter 6

Openness to Change/New Experiences

Openness to Change/New Experiences:

I tend to be:

Extremely High ☐   Very High ☐   High ☐

- Creative

- Artistic or very interested in the arts

- Imaginative

- Curious and interested in new and diverse subjects or people

- Highly attuned to and valuing emotions and gut feelings

- Willing to experiment and try new and exotic things

- Intrigued by and open to different points of view

OR

I tend to be:

Low ☐   Very Low ☐   Extremely Low ☐

- Down-to-earth
- Practical
- More interested in logic than gut feelings and emotions
- Focused on a narrower or more predictable range of interests
- Traditional
- Conservative in my perspectives
- Clear with what I believe is right and wrong

Recall, Openness contrasts those of us who are creative, interested in the arts, imaginative, curious, willing to try new and exotic things, and interested in new and diverse subjects, things and people, with those of us who are more down-to-earth, practical, focused on a narrower range of interests, traditional, and clear about what we believe is right and wrong.

Of the 5 Basic Personality Tendencies, Openness has the least amount of agreement among personality researchers in terms of its importance and measurement.

If you fall somewhere in the middle on Openness, some of the benefits and pitfalls of both high and low levels of this dimension may apply to you. In terms of achievement and success, you'll likely do best by alternating between a focus on change, creativity, and the big picture, and sticking to a tried-and-true routine and mastering it.

THE NEUROSCIENCE OF OPENNESS

Like Extraversion, Openness appears to be related to the sensitivity of the brain's dopamine reward pathways.[19] If you are high on Openness, these reward pathways are likely highly sensitive. Your brain's idling, inner focus or imagination network — known as the Default Mode Network — is likely more easily activated and efficient.[20] EEG research by Con Stough and colleagues has found a positive correlation between high Openness and more of the slower — theta — brain wave activity across the brain.[21] Theta activity has been associated with pleasure-seeking and tends to decrease with age. Because theta production is highest in childhood, Stough and his colleagues postulated that those high on Openness may have retained a somewhat childlike wonderment and open-mindedness about their world.

HIGH OPENNESS

If you are high on Openness, you'll do better with variety in your life and will be bored by repetition. If you are training for a sport, you'll likely stay most motivated when you change your training routine often. In a work environment, you will feel most motivated when you have opportunities to learn and try different strategies, routines, and environments. You'll get off on being creative, using your imagination, and looking at the big picture. You will also probably be more open to less conventional ways of looking at or doing things.

However, having high levels of Openness can become problematic. You may have a tendency to come up with ideas or goals that are impractical. Your sense of direction in life, your career, your goals, or how you see

---

[19] Pecina et al., (2013) DRD2 polymorphisms modulate reward and emotion processing, dopamine neurotransmission and openness to experience. Cortex, 49(3), 877-890.

[20] Beaty et al., (2016). Personality and complex brain networks: The role of openness to experience in default network efficiency. Human Brain Mapping, 37(2), 773–779.

[21] Stough et al, (2001). Psychophysiological correlates of the NEO PI-R Openness, Agreeableness and Conscientiousness: Preliminary results. International Journal of Psychophysiology 41, 87-91.

yourself (your identity) may become easily swayed by new experiences, making it hard to stick with things long enough to accomplish anything.

You may also be so unconventional and non-conforming that you have a hard time working with teams or within organizations, since they may seem too constricting or conventional to you. At the extreme, you may also be prone to excessive daydreaming, fantasizing, or to eccentric ideas such as unsupported alternative therapies like healing with magnets, or unconventional beliefs like the existence of alien abductions. If you're also low on Agreeableness, you may have a particular attraction to conspiracy theories.

Low Openness

If you are low on Openness, you'll likely relish repetition, tradition, or practicality. You'll feel most motivated with a no-fluff or no-nonsense approach that you can learn and then repeatedly put into action. You'll probably feel most comfortable and motivated when you have a trusted coach or mentor giving you a tried-and-true plan of action to take your game to the next level.

Of course, this also can become problematic, as you may find it hard to adapt to changes in routine or other social or personal changes. You may have a hard time understanding and tolerating people with different points of view or lifestyles, especially if you are also low on Agreeableness.

At the end of your athletic career, or if you are forced into a sudden career change due to downsizing or technological advances that make your job obsolete, you may have a hard time finding something else you're interested in because of your narrower set of interests. You may also struggle with using your creativity and imagination to come up with a new career path.

Combinations with Openness

It can be helpful to look at combinations of your Basic Personality Tendencies. For instance, where you fall on the two dimensions of

Openness and Negative Emotions can shed light on some of the ways you may be hard-wired to handle problems and stress.

If you are high on Negative Emotions and low on Openness, you may prefer not to think about problems and stressors when they arise. This may be below your awareness. You may also have a hard time describing your feelings. This style of coping can lead to problems building up before you are aware of them, which can then lead to a sudden breakdown. If this pattern describes you, then you must learn to identify when stress is building up and find ways to deal with it before it becomes a problem. Many of the strategies in the upcoming books in this series will be helpful for you.

If you are high on Negative Emotions and high on Openness, then you may be overly sensitive to problems and stressors, especially if you are also low on Extraversion. You likely have an active imagination that can backfire when problems occur, due to your ability to vividly imagine all the possible ways things can go wrong. If this sounds familiar, you will need to work hard to keep your stress to manageable levels or else you risk burning out.

If you are low on Negative Emotions and low on Openness, you may not experience strong negative emotions or get too caught up in them when faced with problems and stressors. You are more likely to either distract yourself or take practical steps to solve the problem.

If you are low on Negative Emotions and high on Openness and are faced with problems or stressors, you may spend time pondering what these bring up within you and use what you find to inspire you. This may emerge in the form of artistic inspiration and creativity, or in figuring out ways to harness this energy to help you achieve your goals.

Key Takeaways

- Openness contrasts those who are creative, interested in the arts, imaginative, or curious about new and diverse things and people, with those who are more down-to-earth, practical, focused on a narrower range of interests, traditional, and clear with what they believe is right and wrong.

- Openness is the most debated of the 5 Basic Personality Tendencies in terms of its importance and how to measure it.

- If you are high on Openness, you're going to do better with variety in your life and will get bored with repetition. You'll likely stay most motivated when you're learning new things or changing routines and environments. You'll also feel at home when thinking creatively or "outside the box."

- If you are high on this dimension, then you may have a tendency to come up with ideas or goals that are impractical. You may have a hard time settling on one type of career or sticking to a set of goals, and have a hard time in overly traditional or conventional sport or working environments.

- If you are low on Openness, you'll do best in environments that call for repetition, tradition, or practicality. You'll feel most motivated with straightforward and no-nonsense approaches to things that have stood the test of time.

- Drawbacks of low Openness can be difficulties adapting to changes in routine or other shifts. You may also have a hard time understanding and tolerating teammates, colleagues, or superiors with different points of view.

- Where you fall on the two dimensions of Openness and Negative Emotions can shed light on some of the ways you may be hardwired to handle problems and stress and how to overcome them.

Chapter 7

AGREEABLENESS

Agreeableness

I tend to be:

Extremely High ☐   Very High ☐   High ☐

- Quite trusting
- Open and revealing with my thoughts and feelings
- Highly concerned with helping others
- More interested in cooperation over competition
- Lenient towards others' shortcomings
- Deferring to others
- Modest
- Highly sympathetic and easily moved by others' pleas

OR

I tend to be:

Low ☐   Very Low ☐   Extremely Low ☐

- More skeptical and not easily duped

- Guarded with what I share with others

- Focused on my problems and goals

- Self-protective

- Competitive

- Vocal about what I disagree with

- Proud and not afraid to let others know

- Tough-minded and objective

This Basic Personality Tendency dictates your general attitude towards others, from being trusting, open, altruistic, cooperative, modest, and sympathetic to being skeptical, guarded, self-protective, competitive, proud, and tough-minded. Keep in mind that this is different from your level of Extraversion, which has more to do with whether you are attracted to external sources of stimulation, be it social or other.

If you believe you're in the middle with regard to Agreeableness, then you're likely what work personality experts Howard and Howard call a Negotiator.[22] You're more likely to see both sides of the equation, especially in interpersonal situations. You will be able to call upon aspects of both high and low Agreeableness depending on the circumstances.

---

[22] Howard & Howard. The Owner's Manual for Personality at Work: How the Big Five Personality Traits Affect Performance, Communication, Teamwork, Leadership, and Sales: http://goo.gl/OGwh9S

THE NEUROSCIENCE OF AGREEABLENESS

MRI research by DeYoung and his colleagues (2010) has found that high Agreeableness is associated with a smaller posterior left superior temporal sulcus, which is the outer part of your brain just above and behind your left ear.[23] This part of the brain is involved in the interpretation of other peoples' actions and intentions. DeYoung noted that this suggests that people who are high on Agreeableness can use this area of the brain more efficiently.

DeYoung and his colleagues also found that high Agreeableness was associated with a larger posterior cingulate cortex, which is thought to control our ability to understand others' beliefs and adopt their perspectives, which are important for empathy.

Lastly, DeYoung and his colleagues also found an association between Agreeableness and the size of a brain region known as the fusiform gyrus. This area of the brain is related to one's ability to perceive and recognize faces.

Together, these findings support the idea that where you fall on Agreeableness shows up in your brain in areas responsible for processing social information.

HIGH AGREEABLENESS – WHAT IT MEANS FOR YOU

If you are high on Agreeableness, you'll likely do well in team environments, given your tendency to trust and get along well with others. Coaches and managers may like you given that you are a team player and likely put the team's interests above your own. This is especially true if you are also high on Motivation.

---

[23] DeYoung et al. (2010). Testing predictions from personality neuroscience: Brain structure and the Big Five. Psychological Science, 21(6), 820–828.

If this is you, then you are likely to work hard for the benefit of your team or company. You probably channel your motivation, persistence, and self-discipline in order to benefit others. Coaches, teams, managers, and companies love having you on board because of your willingness to take on and complete the hard tasks that nobody wants to do.

If you are also high on Extraversion, then you are warm and agreeable and probably well-liked by others. Others will be able to tell that you care about people, and are a warm and trustworthy friend. You're probably easy to get along with and popular.

On the other hand, if you are high on Agreeableness and low on Negative Emotions, then you're easygoing and unlikely to feel or express too much anger. You're more inclined to let things slide, see both sides of an issue, and move on.

However, if you are high on Agreeableness, you may also be prone to being too cooperative and nice, which can lead others to take advantage of you if you're not careful. You may also have a difficult time standing up to others or showing anger or disapproval when you should.

If you are high on Agreeableness and high on Negative Emotions, then you may be more on the timid side. You may feel a lot of inner conflict, as your feelings are likely easily hurt, but at the same time you're probably reluctant to express your anger because you don't want to offend others.

If you're high on Agreeableness, then you might be too honest and revealing at times. This over-honesty can work against your own success by exposing potential weaknesses that can be taken advantage of in some situations, like when interacting with potential competitors in sports or business. Sometimes it's good to lay all your cards on the table, and sometimes it's best to keep your cards to yourself. The latter is especially true if the other person is low on Agreeableness.

Generally having empathy for others is a good thing. But there is such a thing as having too much empathy which can happen with those who are really high on Agreeableness. This is especially true if you are also high on Negative Emotions, as you may feel others' pain too strongly and over-identify with them. This can affect your objectivity. You may tend to sacrifice your own needs, health, and interests in an attempt to please others, or because you take on too much responsibility for the problems of others.

AGREEABLENESS AND LEADERSHIP

If you are high on Agreeableness and also low on Extraversion, then you may be too unassuming and not assertive enough for leadership roles in sports, business, or the military. You may also have a hard time accepting compliments or acknowledging your own strengths and talents, because you're too modest. Research has generally found that where you fall on Agreeableness predicts leadership ability differently depending on the setting. It turns out that good leaders have a profile of:[24]

- High Extraversion

- High Motivation

- High Openness

- Low Negative Emotions

So, you can be either highly agreeable or disagreeable and still be a good leader. But most effective leaders like high levels of external stimulation, and are extraverted, motivated, self-controlled, open, and don't experience too much negative emotion or get easily rattled by stress. If you want to be a leader and don't have this profile, then you'll have to work on these tendencies.

---

[24] Judge et al. (2002). Personality and leadership: A qualitative and quantitative review. Journal of Applied Psychology, 87(4), 765-780.

Low Agreeableness –
The Good, the Bad, and the Ugly

If you are low on Agreeableness, you tend to be competitive, express your opinions and disagreements, and have an "I don't put up with anything" attitude. You're probably skeptical of others' intentions and pride yourself on your ability to read people, especially their motives. You're likely anything but naive. You probably love to win given your attraction to competition.

The tendencies of those with low Agreeableness can be a great strength in sports and business for obvious reasons. It can also backfire if you are not careful. Too much skepticism, cynicism, and questioning of those who are in a superior position, like your coach or manager, can lead to resentment and simply being disliked. Similarly, while being low on Agreeableness can be adaptive in sport and business, it's usually not very adaptive in close relationships, or in your family life where being skeptical, untrusting, and competitive are usually the opposite of what is called for.

I'm personally somewhat low on Agreeableness. When I was primarily working as an independent evaluator in the fields of forensic and medical-legal psychology, being average-to-low on Agreeableness was a strength. Many of the people I was evaluating were trying to lie and manipulate or fake psychological problems for money or other benefits. It really helped me to be somewhat skeptical, logical, and tough-minded and not passive, naive, or overly trusting. These traits helped me do my job very well.

However, this same set of traits was not at all helpful in my personal and family life. Many of us are often not as aware of our traits as we think we are. I became aware of this tendency in myself with the use of a similar personality measure to the one in this book and with some prompting from my better half. This self-awareness allowed me to catch myself being too disagreeable at times, and then to purposely take it down a notch.

If you are low on Agreeableness, then you need to be aware of and tone down your skepticism, cynicism, competitive nature, combativeness, and even immodesty in circumstances where these are not helpful to you or those around you. You need to be aware that you may come across to others as rude, arrogant, disrespectful, and even manipulative at times. These tendencies will get amplified when you're stressed, tired, and overworked. It may be worth letting others know when you need space and time alone, as this can often be enough to get some perspective.

If you are low on Agreeableness and high on Extraversion, then you may be a good leader in certain situations, given that you are likely dominant and self-assured. You would enjoy making big decisions and directing and managing others. But as noted earlier, most effective leaders are also highly motivated, self-controlled, open, and don't experience too much negative emotion.

If you are low on Agreeableness and high on Motivation, then you are likely to be ambitious and have high standards for yourself *and others*. If you have this profile, then you may be at risk of becoming confrontational when things or people get in the way of your goals. This combination is common in those who are successful climbing their way to the top of a sport or field when you have to be a little ruthless.

One problem that is strongly related to Agreeableness is hostility and anger control. Whether you *feel* a lot of anger and hostility is primarily determined by your standing on Negative Emotions. Whether you *express* your anger is usually a function of where you fall on the Agreeableness spectrum, however. If you're low on both of these dimensions, then you may be a bit cold and callous. You don't get mad, but you do get even. You're probably good at registering wrongdoings done against you, but are able to keep your cool and respond when the time is right. This combination of traits can get you into serious trouble if you're not careful.

THE 'TYPE A' PERSONALITY

You may have heard of the concept of the "Type A Personality." This was developed by two cardiologists in an attempt to validate their perception of the types of patients who appeared to develop coronary artery disease or

CAD. Those with "Type A" personalities were conceptualized as being competitive, ambitious, impatient, aggressive, fast-talking, highly organized, status-focused, and workaholics. Newer, more sophisticated research by psychologists showed that it was really only the tendency towards hostility that predicted heart disease.

If you're high on Negative Emotions and low on Agreeableness, then you are likely at least somewhat temperamental and hostile in that you get pissed off pretty easily and aren't afraid to let others know. This tendency can not only be bad for your relationships, it can also be bad for your heart. Letting others know when you're upset is usually a good thing. But it can become problematic when you lose your composure and do something you regret. You may also take a long time to come down once you're set off.

From a neuropsychological point of view, this is most likely related to what is commonly referred to as the "amygdala hijack", a term coined by Daniel Goleman, whose books popularized the concept of Emotional Intelligence.[25] Recall that your amygdala is a set of almond-shaped structures deep within both sides of your brain that are responsible for negative emotions such as fear and anger. An "amygdala hijack" occurs when your prefrontal cortex is not able to suppress your negative emotions produced by your amygdala, which essentially "hijacks" your prefrontal cortex's ability to think rationally.

STEVE'S TURNAROUND

Many high achievers I've worked with have this profile of high Negative Emotions and low Agreeableness. For example, Steve was a high-ranking military officer who came to see me because he felt that his high levels of stress, which he attributed to what he perceived to be his co-commanders' incompetence, were interfering with his ability to perform up to his

---

[25] Goleman. Emotional Intelligence: Why It Can Matter More Than IQ: http://goo.gl/tnPrIR

potential. He originally wanted to get some advice on how to "put some of them in their place."

It turned out that Steve was high on Negative Emotions and low on Agreeableness. Steve had a bad habit of getting so angry with others at work that he would "see red and lose it." Although he didn't get violent, he would go into a tirade and be angry for hours. He would essentially fall victim to the amygdala hijack and do and say things he later regretted. He also found that he had a hard time calming down and functioning effectively after one of his blowouts.

After discussing Basic Personality Tendencies and having Steve complete a personality measure, he began to realize that a lot of his anger and stress were generated from within himself. He admitted that he had a number of colleagues who also faced the same problems, but did not react the same way he did. Without this realization and understanding of his own personality tendencies, Steve would never have made any further progress toward his goals.

Steve and I worked together for a number of months using the strategies discussed in the upcoming books in this series. We were able to lower his Negative Emotions set-point and help him identify strategies to ensure that he didn't fall victim to amygdala hijacks as often. After doing so, Steve no longer felt like a helpless victim to what was happening around him, and was able to regain control of his life and make progress on his real goals of protecting his country.

Key Takeaways

- The Basic Personality Tendency of Agreeableness refers to our general attitude toward others, ranging from being trusting, open, altruistic, cooperative, modest, and sympathetic to being skeptical, guarded, self-protective, competitive, proud, and tough-minded.

- If you're high on Agreeableness, you'll do well in team environments, given that you're likely a good team player due to your tendency to be trusting, helpful, and easy to get along with.

- High Agreeableness can work to your disadvantage when the situation calls for competition over cooperation, or when you need to be skeptical in your dealings with others who are not looking out for your best interests. In these circumstances, those with low levels of Agreeableness have the advantage.

- If you are high on this dimension, you are at risk of being taken advantage of by others. You may be susceptible to sacrificing your own needs, health, and interests in an attempt to please others, or to taking on others' problems.

- Being low on Agreeableness can also be problematic, since too much skepticism, cynicism, and questioning of those who are in a superior position can lead to resentment, being disliked, or worse.

- Similarly, being low on Agreeableness is usually not very adaptive in close relationships because being skeptical, untrusting, and competitive are usually the opposite of what is called for in such relationships.

- If you are low on Agreeableness and high on Negative Emotions, you'll be prone to be angry and hostile, which can wreak havoc on your relationships and health. This pattern can lead to an "amygdala hijack," which can literally shut down the rational and logical part of your brain, and lead to very bad decisions.

Resources

The Owner's Manual For Personality At Work: How the Big Five Personality Traits Affect Performance, Communication, Teamwork, Leadership, and Sales by Pierce Howard, Ph.D. & Jane Howard, MBA: http://goo.gl/OGwh9S

Chapter 8

MOTIVATION/SELF-CONTROL

Motivation/Self-Control:

I tend to be:

Extremely High ☐   Very High ☐   High ☐

- Self-controlled
- Disciplined
- Competent
- Goal-oriented
- Ambitious and driven
- Detail oriented
- Organized and planful
- Efficient
- Deliberate (take a lot of time to make decisions)

OR

I tend to be:

Low ☐   Very Low ☐   Extremely Low ☐

- Unsure of my abilities
- Inefficient
- Turned off by schedules
- Disorganized
- Undisciplined
- Low in ambition and drive
- Avoidant of big and ambitious goals
- Very spontaneous (make decisions without too much thought)

Recall that the Basic Personality Tendency of Motivation/Self-Control contrasts those of us who are sure of our abilities, organized, detail-oriented, disciplined, goal-oriented, ambitious, and deliberate, with those who are more spontaneous, unsure of our abilities, inefficient, disorganized, undisciplined, and lacking ambition and drive.

If you fall in the middle between high and low Motivation, some of the information related to both extremes will apply to you. You will at times need to improve your motivation, discipline, and ambition. At other times, you may need to pull these back a little and make sure you aren't getting overly perfectionistic, focusing on the wrong things, or burning out. You'll need to be keenly self-aware of these potential pitfalls if you want to make sure you'll achieve your goals.

HIGH MOTIVATION

If you are high on Motivation, you have higher levels of ambition and belief in your ability to accomplish your goals. You're probably good at putting up with pain in the present in order to achieve a long-range goal.

This is related to your brain's executive system. Having a strong executive system means you are good at motivating yourself to do things, controlling your emotions, inhibiting impulses, staying focused, and organizing and planning. Consistent with this, research has found a positive correlation between Motivation and the size of the left lateral prefrontal cortex, an area of the brain that controls our ability to self-regulate.[26]

If you are high on this dimension, then you don't need much help getting motivated to do things that are difficult, as long as you know it's in the best interests of you or your team, company, or family.

As noted earlier in this book, if you are high on Motivation and low on Negative Emotions, you have the personality makeup of a prototypical high achiever. You're likely driven, competent, and self-controlled and rarely derailed by inevitable setbacks you face along the way. You have a significant advantage when it comes to achieving big goals.

DANGER ZONES

If you're high on this dimension and high on Negative Emotions, you are ambitious and driven, but may have a hard time dealing with the unavoidable failures you'll have to confront on your journey to achieve your goals. You will be at increased risk of setting unrealistic and perfectionistic standards. So make sure you're focused on the right things and that you don't become overly perfectionistic in your expectations for yourself.

Don't get me wrong here; you want to have high standards. Many of the high achievers I work with learned from a young age that developing

---

[26] DeYoung et al. (2010). Testing predictions from personality neuroscience: Brain structure and the Big Five. Psychological Science, 21(6), 820 828.

discipline and strong work habits helped them achieve goals. They also learned that, if they raised their standards for performance — the number of goals they can score in a season, grade point averages, or income — they rose to the occasion and achieved goals by meeting their new standards.

The drawback of this approach is they internalize this method of increasing standards to achieve goals and eventually hit a ceiling as they get better and better. At this point, a professional hockey goalie might get angry at himself every time a goal is scored on him and does not get a shutout, his new standard. Or a writer beats herself up if she gets two bad reviews on Amazon.com despite having 50 good reviews!

Given their new unattainable, or at least unsustainable, standard of perfection, their belief in themselves can deflate every time they fail to live up to it. This mindset is a recipe for failure. You need to be aware of this and realize that perfectionistic standards are now hurting, rather than helping you.

If you are high on Motivation, you can end up working too hard and burn yourself out in the false belief that more is better. You're at risk of workaholism. You may become so focused on getting things done that you neglect other areas in your life that you value, like your health, relationships, family, and even just taking time to relax, play or enjoy a hobby. You're probably a planner by nature, so you should consider scheduling some down time, along with time with family, friends, and hobbies. Many of the stress-management strategies in the upcoming books in this series will also be important to develop.

You may also be at risk of missing the forest for the trees, or getting lost in the details. I'm definitely high on Motivation and can say that I have fallen victim to working really hard without taking a step back to make sure I was working hard on the right things.

One example of this was my work in the forensic psychology and medical-legal arena. I started doing this type of work in graduate school for a highly respected and sought-after forensic psychologist to gain more experience and to help pay the bills. I worked really hard and excelled at this. It took me a few years to realize that I was working really hard on the wrong things for me. I started doing the forensic work to broaden my understanding of human nature and to challenge myself by working with difficult people. I was repeatedly reinforced by getting more and more opportunities to do this type of work for more and more money.

As time went on, I started to realize I was not following my original passions and reasons for entering the field of psychology. It took hard work and the use of many of the strategies in this book for me to wake up and realize I was heading down the wrong path.

If you are high on Motivation and you too have found yourself working too hard on the wrong things, then the exercises in this book will be very important for you. These exercises should be repeated at least once a year, if not more often, to make sure you are on the right path. These strategies will help you stay focused on the right things.

LOW MOTIVATION

If you are low on the Basic Personality Tendency of Motivation, then you may struggle with staying disciplined, focused on your goals, and feeling competent at times. You likely have weaker executive abilities that serve to help you control yourself, stay focused, inhibit impulses, motivate yourself to do things, and organize and plan.[27]

You may even have too much slow brain-wave activity in the front half of your brain, similar to that seen in most people diagnosed with Attention Deficit/Hyperactivity Disorder (ADHD/ADD). Consistent with this, research by Stough and colleagues found, the personality dimension of Motivation was negatively correlated with slow, theta wave, brain activity in the frontal regions of the brain, which is often used as a diagnostic marker

---

[27] Forbes et al. (2014). The role of executive function and the dorsolateral prefrontal cortex in the expression of neuroticism and conscientiousness. Social Neuroscience, 9(2), 139-151.

for ADHD.[28] Research has also consistently found an association between the Basic Personality Tendency of Motivation and ADHD.[29] Of course, although most people with ADHD are low on Motivation, most people with low levels of Motivation do not have ADHD.

There is some evidence that we can improve executive functions such as our attention and working memory through things like cognitive brain training programs.[30] There is even more evidence that if you do have too much slow brain-wave activity, this too can be improved with something called neurofeedback, which will be discussed in more detail in the upcoming books in this series. In fact, there is a lot of evidence that neurofeedback is effective in helping those with ADHD/ADD or tendencies toward such difficulties.[31] I must note that I'm not aware of any studies showing changes in the Basic Personality Tendency of Motivation in response to neurofeedback. But theoretically, I believe it may improve certain aspects of this dimension such as attention, impulse control, motivation, and planning.

Similarly, there is accumulating evidence that neurofeedback is effective in improving various types of performances such as musical performances and, especially, sport-related performance.[32,33]

---

[28] Stough et al. (2001). Psychophysiological correlates of the NEO PI-R Openness, Agreeableness and Conscientiousness: Preliminary results. International Journal of Psychophysiology, 41, 87-91.

[29] Parker et al. (2004). ADHD symptoms and personality: Relationships with the Five Factor Model of personality. Personality and Individual Differences, 36, 977–987.

[30] Smith et al. (2009). A cognitive training program based on principles of brain plasticity: Results from the Improvement in Memory with Plasticity-based Adaptive Cognitive Training Study. Journal of the American Geriatrics Society. 57(4), 594–603.

[31] Martijn et al. (2014). Evaluation of neurofeedback in ADHD: The long and winding road. Biological Psychology, 95, 108-115.

[32] Gruzelier (2014). EEG-neurofeedback for optimising performance. I: A review of cognitive and affective outcome in healthy participants. Neuroscience and Biobehavioral Reviews, 44, 124-141.

[33] Gruzelier (2014). EEG-neurofeedback for optimising performance. II: Creativity, the performing arts and ecological validity. Neuroscience and Biobehavioral Reviews, 44, 142-158.

If you are a high achiever who is trying to do everything in your power to get to the next level, then you at least have to try a course of neurofeedback and see what happens. More on this in the upcoming books in this series.

LOW MOTIVATION AND YOUR HEALTH

If you are low on this Basic Personality Tendency, then you are also at the highest risk for negative health outcomes. Many of the diseases that affect us in the modern world are preventable to a large extent through things like diet, exercise, and avoidance of chemicals and carcinogens such as cigarettes and alcohol. These are all things that require motivation, willpower, and self-control to regularly engage in or avoid. Your standing on Motivation is a strong predictor of how long you'll live.[34] Also, those with low Motivation and high Negative Emotions are at the greatest risk for problems like gambling and substance abuse.[35] Of course, this means that although many people with these types of problems have this personality profile, most people with this profile don't have problems with gambling or substance abuse.

Not surprisingly, poor health, gambling, and substance abuse are going to pose formidable problems when it comes to your success. So knowing where you stand on these dimensions and then doing something about it is essential to maximizing your potential.

LOW MOTIVATION AND ACHIEVEMENT

Achieving big goals is going to be an uphill battle for those who are low on the Basic Personality Tendency of Motivation. For those low on this dimension, the risk of underachievement is high. In other words, you're

---

[34] Hill et al. (2011). Conscientiousness and longevity: An examination of possible mediators. Health Psychology, 30(5), 536-541.

[35] Bogg & Roberts (2004). Conscientiousness and health-related behaviors: A meta-analysis of the leading behavioral contributors to mortality. Psychological Bulletin, 130(6), 887-919.

likely an underachiever in the sense that you may have strengths and potential that are not being fully utilized.

If you are low on Motivation and low on Negative Emotions, you tend not to be interested in achieving high levels of what society typically defines as "success." You probably have a care-free, ultra-relaxed, and laid-back lifestyle and demeanour. But if you happen to have this profile and have some big goals you want to achieve, then the strategies in this book will be essential to get you motivated to do something that is meaningful for you.

If on the other hand, you are low on Motivation and high on Negative Emotions, you likely avoid competitive or achievement situations like the plague. You may have a strong fear not only of success, but also failure. You probably often feel like you're at the mercy of your own impulses because you feel unable to resist urges and desires. You likely have a hard time stopping yourself from doing things you know you shouldn't be doing, which is usually due to difficulties controlling your emotions. You also have a hard time getting yourself to do things you know you should be doing, which is due to difficulties with motivation. To achieve big goals, you will have to work very hard staying disciplined and focused.

THE ENFORCER

I once worked with a professional hockey player whose primary role through much of his professional hockey career was as an "enforcer." For those of you not familiar with hockey, each team has about 1 to 3 enforcers whose primary role is to protect teammates and to drop the gloves and take on the opposing team's enforcer to lift morale. This player, we'll call him Denis, had the Basic Personality Tendency profile of low Motivation and high Negative Emotions. You may wonder how someone with low Motivation could make it to a professional level. As will be outlined more below, these individuals tend to achieve more when they are in highly structured work environments that essentially serve as their prefrontal cortex to reduce the load on their executive functions, which keeps them in check and on track.

Given Denis' personality profile, it was not surprising that his role was to fight at the drop of a hat (or glove). It didn't hurt that he was somewhat low on Agreeableness as well. Denis came to me because of problems off the ice. Specifically, he became addicted to pain killers he began taking after knee surgery a year or so before we met. He didn't need them for pain anymore, but kept using them and felt he couldn't stop. It turned out he was using them as a way to control his negative emotions and deal with the inevitable stresses that come along with being a professional athlete.

Denis and I worked together for a while, but he first needed to safely withdraw from the painkillers under medical supervision. He did so and then we got to work. Not surprisingly, given his low standing on Motivation, Denis had a hard time doing any "homework" between sessions. But using many of the strategies in this book, we worked on building up his WHY for completing the between-session assignments. We then got to work on two main tasks.

One was helping him learn to better control his negative emotions and stress through strategies that included changes in diet, sleep, light exposure, and his thinking patterns. We also worked on improving his stress response through Heart Rate Variability training, improving his ability to inhibit his impulses through computerized cognitive training, and improving his ability to regulate his mental states through EEG neurofeedback training. For those of you interested in learning more, I will go into much more detail in the upcoming books in this series.

The second major focus was on designing his environment so that various temptations were minimized, which helped him keep his willpower tank from running near empty. There will be more on willpower in the last section of this book.

Denis was able to stay off painkillers and regulate his emotions much better. His performance improved on the ice in that he took fewer unnecessary penalties and generally felt more in control of himself. His personal life also improved. He learned that he would have to change his lifestyle by incorporating many of the above strategies into his daily life permanently if he was going to function at his best.

CONTROL YOUR ENVIRONMENT OR BE CONTROLLED

As noted, if you are low on the Motivation dimension, you may do well when you have an environment (e.g., team, training schedule, or job) that is highly organized for you. Using your willpower in the face of having too much choice (e.g., whether to get up at 6 a.m. to train) will be hard. If the environment is already organized for you, then making the right choice will be easier.

For example, one strategy for this is called stimulus control which I alluded to when discussing Denis earlier. To see this in action, take the example of having a difficult time getting yourself to stop eating junk food at night. If you tend to overeat on junk food at night, you would make it really hard to get your hands on junk food by removing it from the house.

Or if you want to get up at 6 a.m. to work out or work on a project, you can make it easier by having things prepared the evening before. For example, you would get all of your workout clothes, equipment, water, and gear laid out and ready to go the night before. When you wake up the next day, the experience is less painful and demanding on your limited willpower.

Many of the strategies in this book will also be helpful in improving your discipline, focus on goals, and feelings of competence. For example, the Funeral, Values Clarification, and the Process vs. Outcome Goals exercises will be essential to keep you motivated toward achieving your goals.

Key Takeaways

- The Basic Personality Tendency of Motivation contrasts those of us who are sure of our abilities, organized, detail-oriented, disciplined, goal-oriented, ambitious, and deliberate with those who are more spontaneous, unsure of our abilities, inefficient, disorganized, undisciplined, and lacking in ambition and drive.

- Where you stand on this personality dimension is related to your prefrontal cortex, executive system, and possibly the amount of your slow-wave brain activity.

- If you are high on Motivation, then you tend to have high levels of motivation, ambition and belief in your ability to accomplish your goals.

- Drawbacks of high Motivation include being at risk of missing the forest for the trees, having perfectionistic standards, and becoming a workaholic. The exercises in this book will help prevent these from occurring.

- If you are low on Motivation, then you struggle to stay disciplined, focused on your goals, and feeling competent at times.

- If you are low on this dimension, your set point may be changeable by improving your executive functions, and your ability to focus and inhibit impulses using cognitive brain training and neurofeedback. The strategies in this book will also help you find your purpose or mission and put this into action, which will serve to keep you motivated and moving forward.

Chapter 9

STEP 1: KNOW YOURSELF - CONCLUSION

At this point, you should know a lot more about where you land on the 5 Basic Personality Tendencies. These are based on over 65 years of research by some of psychology's best and brightest minds. We all fall somewhere along the continuum on each of these.

You also learned how your specific personality traits can be strengths and weaknesses. Knowledge is power. With this knowledge of your and others' personality alone, you are light years ahead of 99 percent of the population in terms of understanding how we tick.

You now know your personality hardware. You know more about What you are. As useful as this information is, it's only the first step toward understanding who you are, what you really want, and how to achieve the right goals for you.

Our basic personality is hard to change without a lot of work. As a first step, you need to become aware of your basic personality by completing the brief measure in Chapter 3. The more extreme your scores are on one side or the other for each basic tendency, the more difficult it will be for you to alter this natural way of being for more than a short period of time.

Remember, your basic personality is both a strength and weakness, depending on your environment, lifestyle, values, and goals. When you fall at the extremes, it may be in your best interest to try to mitigate these basic tendencies in situations where they are not helpful. In other circumstances, these can be strengths and you need to be aware of this so you can capitalize on them.

In the next section, you're going to learn a little more about your software, or what's important to you. These are your values. As Tony Robbins declared, "Success without fulfillment is the ultimate failure." You can't be fulfilled if you are successful at things that are not in line with your deepest values. You're pretty much guaranteed to underperform if you are working on achieving things that are not in line with what's truly important to you. So let's keep the momentum going and get you more connected with what's really important to you.

STEP 2

KNOW YOUR VALUES

Chapter 10

KNOW HOW YOU
WANT TO LIVE YOUR LIFE

It's not hard to make decisions when you know what your values are.
— Roy Disney

Your beliefs become your thoughts,
Your thoughts become your words,
Your words become your actions,
Your actions become your habits,
Your habits become your values,
Your values become your destiny.
— Mahatma Gandhi

You should now know a lot more about your basic makeup, your Basic Personality Tendencies and how they are both strengths and weaknesses essential to your success. But this is only the first step.

You need to know more about who and what you are, what's important to you and how you want to live your life. Living a life incongruent with your own deeper values is a recipe for failure.

As noted earlier in this book, there is nothing worse than going through years of blood, sweat, and tears pursuing a goal only to realize that you were focusing on the wrong goal, or a goal that was incongruent with what you truly value.

When we live a life incongruent with our Basic Personality Tendencies and values, we are likely to become depressed, anxious, and possibly addicted to substances to get by. Don't let this be you! With a few simple exercises, you can prevent this from happening.

PERSONALITY TENDENCIES AND VALUES ARE NOT THE SAME THING

Your Basic Personality Tendencies were not chosen by you – they are hard-wired into your brain due to a combination of your genes and your experiences in life, especially when you were growing up. Your Basic Personality Tendencies are changeable to a certain extent, but they are not easily altered. They generally stay with you your entire life.

Your values on the other hand, are developed through your experiences, such as how you were raised or socialized. Values tend to change over time and they can be more easily changed by new experiences and be chosen by you.

Your personality and values can at times seem to be incongruent. For example, you can value calm and stability, but have a personality style that makes you susceptible to negative emotions and stress. Or you can value achievement, success, and hard work, but be low on the personality dimension of Motivation.

The trick is to know what your Basic Personality Tendencies and values are. I can't overstate this enough. Living a life incongruent with your values will lead you down a path of failure and unhappiness. And without the knowledge and strategies to work with or around your Basic Personality Tendencies, you will never reach goals that are truly in line with your values.

HOW ARE TENDENCIES AND VALUES RELATED?

There are a couple Basic Personality Tendency profiles that can influence the type of values you have. These are primarily related to where you fall on Openness and Agreeableness.

- Those who are high on both of these personality dimensions tend to value independence and cooperation. You are more likely to believe in the good in people and that through creative and benevolent means, progress can be made to solve society's problems.

- For those who are low on both Openness and Agreeableness, valuing tradition, pragmatism, and realism is more common. You're likely to have strong beliefs about what is right and what is wrong and have little tolerance for those who don't see the world as you do.

- If you are high on Openness and low on Agreeableness, you likely value freedom and unconventionality. You are also unlikely to be swayed by sentimentality or tradition. You are likely open to different views of right and wrong, but once you decide where you stand, you probably don't worry too much if your stance bothers others.

- If you are low on Openness and high on Agreeableness you are likely to value tradition and heritage. You're likely to put a lot of faith in what has been done before and to believe this is the key to the success of families, groups, teams, and society.

There are numerous other ways your Basic Personality Tendencies can influence your values. Below are some examples:

- High Negative Emotions = likely to value order and stability

- High Agreeableness = likely to value cooperation

- Low Agreeableness = likely to value competition

- High Motivation = likely to value achievement

Again, these are not hard-and-fast rules; I'm only pointing these out so you're aware of how your Basic Personality Tendencies may be influencing your perceived values. Sometimes what you value is being driven more by your personality than a conscious choice of what is truly important to you. For example, your high levels of Negative Emotions may be the driving force behind your valuing of order and stability due to a propensity to feel uncomfortable with change and unpredictability. It could be that if you lowered your natural set point on Negative Emotions or learned strategies to prevent your negative emotions from holding you back, you would actually value more excitement and adventure.

Again, the point here is to realize that values can be chosen, but are definitely influenced by things like your Basic Personality Tendencies.

OTHER SOURCES OF OUR VALUES

The late Stephen R. Covey said it best with "Begin with the end in mind." What he meant was, before we decide what to focus on in our lives, we need to find out what is truly important to us. In other words, we need to figure out what our values are. The problem is that this is not as easy as it sounds.

You see, the modern world is engineered to make you value things that may not be a true value for you. Think of all the constant advertisements that we are bombarded with on a daily basis. Marketing departments' main job is to convince you that you value their product, the type of person that uses their product, or the lifestyle their product represents.

These attempts at shaping our values are becoming more and more subtle. What some people don't realize is that simple things like what brand of clothing celebrities or other influencers wear, what car they drive, what accessories or smartphone they carry, and even what they eat and drink are often forms of subtle advertising. Many of these people are paid to be seen using these products. Even people on reality TV shows, who we often don't think of as "celebrities" in the traditional sense, are often paid to wear certain clothes or consume certain brands of soda in the hope that we also will want to use that product.

Even when it comes to careers, society as a whole inadvertently tries to convince us that certain callings are more valued and desirable, with becoming a medical doctor valued over other careers like being a writer. So figuring out what you really value is a lot harder than it seems.

How do We Clarify Our Values?

The reality is most of us live our lives without much thought given to the fact that one day we are going to die. And we avoid thinking about this sort of thing for a good reason. It would be pretty frightening and depressing if we were constantly, acutely aware of our mortality.

But sometimes life throws us a curveball that makes us realize that life is short. Maybe it's the death of a family member or friend. Or maybe it's a health scare. As uncomfortable as these situations are, they can help us live better by helping us start living our lives more in line with our deeper values.

The good news is you don't have to wait for a tragic event to get in touch with what's truly important to you. There are a number of exercises you can do to put things into perspective and clarify your values. These are so helpful that similar exercises have been included in many self-help books such as *The 7 Habits of Highly Effective People*. Such exercises are also used in some of the most powerful forms of psychotherapy, including Acceptance and Commitment Therapy (ACT) and Existential Psychotherapy.

What follows is one of the most effective strategies. Be forewarned, this can be a powerful and oftentimes emotionally difficult experience for many, so be prepared.

How Death Can Help You Find Your Values: The Funeral Exercise

Take a moment and think about how old you will be exactly five years from today. Now imagine in vivid detail you are witnessing your own funeral. You are able to walk around but nobody can see or hear you. Use all of your senses to make this as real as possible. So this means imagining not only what you see and hear, but what it feels like to be in your body, and even what you smell. The more senses you engage, the more real and effective this exercise will be.

Now imagine that a member of your family stood up and gave a speech about you and your life. This could be your significant other, child, parent, or sibling. They are talking about the story of your life, how you were as a child, teenager, and adult. They are describing your accomplishments and setbacks and how you dealt with them. They are especially talking about what you were like as a person. What you did with your time. How you treated others. What was important to you.

Imagine and then write down exactly what you would *__like them to be saying about you and your life.__* Be detailed here. Just let the ideas flow. Imagine this as vividly as possible and fill in the form below:

1. Who is the family member?

_____

2. What are they saying about your accomplishments?

_____

_____

3. What are they saying about your setbacks and how you dealt with them?

_____

_____

4. What are they saying about what you were like as a person?

_____

_____

5. What are they saying about how you spent your time?

_____

_____

6. What are they saying about how you treated others?

_____

_____

7. What are they saying about what was important to you?

_____

_____

8. What are they saying about your legacy?

_____

_____

Now, do this same exercise again, but this time one of your peers, teammates, or colleagues is giving the speech. Imagine this as vividly as possible and fill in the form below:

1. Who is this peer, teammate, or colleague?

_____

2. What are they saying about your accomplishments?

_____

_____

3. What are they saying about your setbacks and how you dealt with them?

_____

_____

4. What are they saying about what you were like as a person?

_____

_____

5. What are they saying about how you spent your time?

_____

_____

6. What are they saying about how you treated others?

_____

_____

7. What are they saying about what was important to you?

_____

_____

8. What are they saying about your legacy?

_____

_____

If you took this exercise seriously and did it properly, you should have felt some strong emotions. It should also help get you into the right mindset to get in touch with what is really important to you. It should give you some perspective on things, what you need to change, what you need to do more of, and what your true values are.

If you took this exercise seriously, you also may have noticed that some of the things that you thought were really important to you didn't come up. Maybe making a million dollars didn't come up. Or you may be realizing that how you're currently spending your time and energy is not congruent with what you just learned about yourself doing the exercise above. This is important information that you need to keep in mind as you complete the rest of the exercises in this book.

VALUES SURVEY

The next exercise is another way to help you get in touch with your deepest values in terms of what is most important to you as a person. I developed this measure based on my own experience working with high achievers and in consultation with the work and measures developed by others.[36]

Clarifying your values will help make sure you're living your life and setting goals congruent with what is most important to you. Too many of us go through life without serious thought about our values and whether we're living our lives congruent with these values.

Visit FriesenPerformance.com/Achieve-Bonus-Materials to download printable copies of the Values Survey.

Values Survey Instructions:

- The goal of this exercise is to help you clarify what is important to you.

- There are no right or wrong answers.

- First read through the list of values below without marking any of the values.

---

[36] The Values Survey was developed based on my own experience working with high achievers and in consultation with the work and measures developed by:
- Shalom Schwartz, Ph.D. (the world's leading research expert on values).
- Pierce Howard, Ph.D. and Jane Howard M.B.A. (from the Center for Applied Cognitive Studies).
- Jeffrey Auerbach, Ph.D. (one of North America's top executive coaches).
- Russ Harris, M.D. (psychiatrist, best-selling author, and one of the world's foremost providers of training in Acceptance and Commitment Therapy).

- Read through a second time. This time **circle** your top 5 to 10 values. There is no need to rank or order these, unless you feel it would be helpful.

- You may find it hard to decide which values to choose. Many of these values are desirable. Think about what is important to you or what you would like to be guiding values in your life. Based on what you learned about yourself from the Funeral Exercise, you can also think about what values you believe will be important to you in the future.

- Some of the values have multiple descriptors. You don't have to value all of them.

- These are for you and you only. So be as honest with yourself as you can.

- If there are values that are important to you but are not listed, write them down in the Other option at the bottom. The list below is not exhaustive. There are many other types of values not included.

Independence/Self-
Direction/Freedom

Fun/Pleasure/Stimulation/Play

Having/Searching
for a Larger Meaning

Leaving a Legacy
for Future Generations

Harmonious Social Relationships

Being Kind/Friendly/
Helpful/Supportive

Contributing/Giving Back

Social Justice/Fairness

Hard Work/Industriousness/
Persistence/Productivity

Success/Accomplishment/
Achievement

Learning/Growing/Improving

Peace/Quiet

Self-Expression

Activity/Intensity/Energy

Skepticism/Keeping
the World Accountable

Honesty/Authenticity

Competition/Winning

Status/Recognition

Prestige

Influencing Others

Adventure/Excitement

Health/Fitness

Courage/Bravery

Loyalty/Trustworthiness

Creativity

Art/Beauty

Personal Safety/Security/Stability

Regional/National Security/Stability

Spirituality

Tradition

Family

Luxury

Wealth/Money

Protecting the Environment

Nature

Inner Calm

Wisdom/Knowledge

Other:_____

Other:_____

Other:_____

Now, look back at your top 5 to 10 values that you circled. Look at one value at a time. For each one, ask yourself:

Am I living my life in line with these values?

If your answer is "yes," then great! Keep up the great work.

If your answer is "no" or "sort of", you need to take a look at your priorities.

Keep in mind, you don't have to be living congruent with your values every day or even every month. You may highly value Art/Beauty but have little time to engage this value due to the fact that other values are taking priority at this point in your life. So you may have a start-up and are working long hours trying to get your product ready for launch next month. Even though you value Art/Beauty, you choose to put this value to the side for now. There's nothing wrong with that. The key is to be aware that you are doing it and then freely choose to do so.

On the other hand, you may highly value Health/Fitness and realize that for the past year, you've been too busy to engage in any health-enhancing activities. Maybe you've stopped working out or almost exclusively eat fast food. You should ask yourself if you need to make some changes to your priorities. Living your life incongruent with your values for long periods of time can lead to unhappiness, stress, and under-performance.

Because our values change over time, it's important to complete this measure about once a year. Mark it on your calendar. Most people find it easiest to do this in early January of each year. Start off each year fresh and in line with what's most important to you.

CONCLUSION

You now have a better understanding of your Basic Personality Tendencies and have connected with your basic values. Some of you may feel like you know yourself a lot better now, but are still not sure what you should be doing in terms of your career or life focus. Or you may want to know if the career you're in or the main focus in your life is right for you. The next step to help figure this out is to get a better sense of your strengths, including your talents, skills, and interests. The next section of this book will systematically help you clarify these to ensure you are on the right path.

BONUS MATERIAL

Visit FriesenPerformance.com/Achieve-Bonus-Materials to download printable copies of the Values Survey.

STEP 3

KNOW YOUR STRENGTHS

Chapter 11

KNOW YOUR TALENTS, SKILLS & INTERESTS

A winner is someone who recognizes his God-given talents, works his tail off to develop them into skills, and uses these skills to accomplish his goals.
— Larry Bird

Your work is going to fill a large part of your life, and the only way to be truly satisfied is to do what you believe is great work. And the only way to do great work is to love what you do. If you haven't found it yet, keep looking. Don't settle. As with all matters of the heart, you'll know when you find it.
— Steve Jobs

Now that you've gotten in touch with what's truly important to you, we have to hone in on your strengths, including your talents, skills, and interests. You can't effectively figure out what you should be focusing on without first knowing your Basic Personality Tendencies and what is truly important to you.

So if you skimmed over the last chapters without doing any of the exercises, I'm just going to come out and say it. You're making a mistake.

You can't make and achieve big goals if they aren't in line with your personality and what is truly important to you.

The next step in this journey is to get in touch with your strengths and passions. This section focuses on figuring out what you are good at and what really interests you.

Keep in mind that being good at something doesn't mean you value the activity or that you're interested in doing it. I've seen this more often than I'd like with high-level athletes. Remember Leroy from Chapter 1? He's the talented and skilled basketball player who could have made the NBA, but fizzled out. It turned out that he didn't really value the lifestyle of playing professional basketball and wasn't really passionate about the game.

So keep this in mind. Knowing your strengths is important for maximizing your potential. But, if you engage these strengths in career trajectories that are not in line with your personality, values, or interests, you are not going to be happy and effective. The key to success is knowing all of these things about yourself and then making sure you're doing something that satisfies as many of them as possible.

Something else to keep in mind is that your personality, values, and interests can also be considered among your strengths. Your talents and skills are more specific, but are strengths as well. Maybe you're skilled at writing. Or maybe you have a talent for reading people. Knowing this about yourself is imperative to your success.

DON'T TRY THIS ON YOUR OWN!

We are usually pretty good judges when it comes to our values and interests. But sometimes we are not the best judges of our strengths, talents, and skills. Often we need feedback from others to see them.

Below is an exercise that many of my clients have found helpful. This exercise helps ensure that you are not discounting anything that you may be blind to when it comes to recognizing your strengths, talents, and skills.

Contact at least 3 to 5 people that know you well. These can be family members, friends, or colleagues. Ask them to honestly answer the questions below. Instead of asking them over the phone or in person, it's usually best to have them take their time and write their responses out on paper or via email. That way, they have time to think about their responses and will be more likely to give you honest and valuable feedback.

In your email, let these people know that you are examining your goals or career options and looking for honest feedback from trusted family, friends, and colleagues. In your email, ask them the following:

1. What do you see as my strengths, talents, and skills?

2. What type of work or career do you think I would be best at and why?

3. Do you think I have strengths, talents, or skills that I may not be aware or? If so, what are they?

Of course, you shouldn't change your goals, career plans, or aspirations simply based on what these people say. Like everything in this book, these are just exercises that will help you develop clarity as to what you should be focusing on.

DISCOVERING YOUR STRENGTHS: GUIDED DISCOVERY EXERCISE

Once you've received feedback from those who know you well, you're ready to start the Strengths Guided Discovery Exercise. This is a culmination of some of the most powerful questions you can ask yourself to get in touch with your strengths, talents, and skills. There is no scoring key, or right or wrong answers. This should be considered a process exercise, in that taking the time to think deeply about these questions will give you ideas, insights, and new perspectives on yourself and what your strengths, talents, and skills really are.

Visit <u>FriesenPerformance.com/Achieve-Bonus-Materials</u> to download printable copies of Strengths Guided Discovery Exercise.

Find a time and place where you can do this without interruption for at least 15 to 30 minutes. Turn off your phone, computer, TV, and put a Do Not Disturb sign on your door if you have to.

First, take 10 slow and long breaths. To do this, breathe in through your nose for 5 seconds and then blow out through your mouth for another 5 seconds. Don't take the deepest breaths possible. Rather, take slow and long breaths. Do it slow enough so that you can stretch it over the entire 10 second breath cycle (in and out). You should focus on the act of breathing. This should result in a mental state of calm focus and help clear your mind before you begin.

Now write down your responses to the following questions:

1. Throughout your schooling, which classes/subjects did you do best in?

_____

2. What was it about the classes/subjects that you enjoyed?

_____

_____

_____

3. Throughout your schooling, which classes/subjects did you struggle with?

_____

4. What was it about the classes/subjects that caused you to struggle?

_____

_____

_____

5. What types of groups or work settings do you feel you fit into best?

_____

_____

_____

6. What groups or work settings do you feel you fit into the least?

_____

_____

_____

7. What activities make you feel like time is moving by slowly and painfully?

_____

_____

_____

8. What kinds of activities give you the feeling of being in the zone (e.g., when you don't notice time and it seems to fly by)?

_____

_____

_____

9. In what activities do you feel most like yourself, when it feels natural to be doing what you're doing?

_____

_____

_____

10. What activities lead you to feel exhausted or tired relatively quickly? (Think more about stress and mental energy as opposed to physically draining activities like housework)

_____

_____

_____

11. What activities can you do without noticing fatigue? When it feels effortless?

_____

_____

_____

12. What do you do better than anything else?

_____

_____

_____

13. Do you have any strengths, talents, or skills you haven't developed but wished you had?

_____

_____

_____

14. Do you have any strengths, talents, or skills you were discouraged from developing?

_____

_____

_____

15. Which strengths, talents, or skills do you think you could really develop if you tried?

_____

_____

_____

16. What do you feel your natural strengths, talents, or skills are?

_____

_____

_____

Once you've done this exercise, ask yourself:

- What did I learn about myself and my strengths, talents, and skills?

- Is there any way to tie in what I discovered in this process with what I am currently focusing on in my life?

- Is there any way to tie in what I discovered in this process with what I can focus on in the future?

- Is there some action I can take to look into the possibility of incorporating more of these strengths, talents, and skills into my current focus or future focus?

Now put it away for at least a full day. Then come back to what you wrote and follow the breathing instructions again. Review what you've written and see what kind of reactions you get when you read it for the second time. Note any new insights or ideas.

KNOW YOUR INTERESTS

Your interests tell you what subjects, activities, or careers you're interested in. If you are looking to change career paths or figure out your career path, then all the exercises in this book are essential. If you are unsure about what you are passionate about, then there are a few more steps you can take to help you develop a clearer picture of what you should do.

If you're an elite or professional athlete, you may think that you should skip this section. Please don't. It's never too early to start thinking about what you want to do when your career ends. Doing this work will help you open your mind to various possibilities. If you know yourself well and have an idea of what you want to do in the future, then your mind will be primed for opportunities and experiences that may help you along your path.

If you're already working in a career that you are sure is well-suited to you in terms of your personality, values, strengths, and interests, then you may want to skip this section.

If you aren't quite satisfied with your current career, are considering a career change, or are just interested in learning more about your career interests, then the exercises below will help you.

When it comes to figuring out what you should be doing as a career, you may want to take a step back to make sure your goals are realistic. Don't get me wrong, I'm all for dreaming big. But if you are a 25-year-old mediocre basketball player who is only 4-foot-11, I think we need to get realistic and realize that a career as an NBA guard is out of the question.

Then again, if you really love basketball, are high in Extraversion and love talking to anyone that will listen to you about basketball, then you might channel that passion into something like your own podcast where you interview people and talk about everything related to basketball. Then the sky is the limit for you.

WHAT ABOUT IQ?

Of course, we have to be realistic as the previous example highlights. But some people think they aren't smart enough to go into certain careers. Of course, one's intelligence is important. It has been found to be related to many important educational, occupational, economic, and social outcomes.

In response to a number of misunderstandings by the public and the mainstream media regarding intelligence, 52 intelligence researchers signed a statement that was published in the scientific journal Intelligence and the Wall Street Journal in 1994.[37,38] In this statement, they jointly defined intelligence as:

---

[37] Gottfredson (1994). Mainstream science on intelligence. Wall Street Journal, December 13, 1994, A18.

[38] Gottfredson (1997). Mainstream science on intelligence: An editorial with 52 signatories, history, and bibliography. Intelligence, 24(1), 13-23.

"A very general mental capability that, among other things, involves the ability to reason, plan, solve problems, think abstractly, comprehend complex ideas, learn quickly and learn from experience."

They go on to note that intelligence "...is not merely book learning, a narrow academic skill, or test-taking smarts. Rather, it reflects the broader and deeper capability for comprehending our surroundings – 'catching on,' 'making sense' of things, or figuring out what to do."

You can think of intelligence as the raw informational processing power of your brain. People with higher IQs find it easier to grasp new information, compare that new information to their existing store of information, and use that information or their sheer reasoning power to solve problems. Having a high IQ is an advantage in life, while having a low IQ is often a disadvantage. The advantages of having a high IQ become more apparent as the complexity of the job or activity increases.

Our intellectual power is reflected in the hard-wiring of our brains. Having a high IQ is like having a lot of RAM and hard-drive space, in addition to a fast CPU. You can also think of it like having a Ferrari engine.

Like our Basic Personality Tendencies, our raw mental powers are partially inherited. Although not impossible to alter, just like our physical skills and muscle composition, there appears to be an upper limit as to how much we can improve our IQ with today's knowledge and technologies. But the information presented in this series of books will help you to maximize your brain and body's capabilities.

Although having a high IQ is an advantage when it comes to success, it really depends on who's behind the wheel. Success depends on a combination of things. Even for what are traditionally considered the more intellectually advanced professions like law, medicine, engineering, and academia, having an IQ in the superior range is not a prerequisite.

Of course, a superior IQ will make certain aspects of these occupations, particularly the learning part, easier and faster. But most are surprised to hear that even in these "brainy" careers, you only need about average intelligence to succeed. In fact, about 50 percent of the population has an IQ high enough to succeed in these careers.

If you are reading this book and understand the majority of what is written, then you are most likely within this group of people. What's really important is whether you work hard and whether you work intelligently. Your drive is what really matters. Your drive depends on whether your goals and mission are in line with your deepest values. As Nietzsche said, "He who has a why to live can bear almost any how."

HOW YOUR BASIC PERSONALITY TENDENCIES INFLUENCE YOUR CAREER INTERESTS

Knowing your Basic Personality Tendencies, what's truly important to you, and your strengths are essential for your success. But many of you may be unsure whether your career path is right for you. Or you may be unsure what type of career you should pursue. The next step is for you to get in touch with your career interests.

Being a trained psychologist, I'm partial to psychological measures as you may have already noticed. I've been providing in-depth career assessments for many different types of people for many years now. These people include those with traumatic brain injuries, physical injuries, or psychological difficulties. On the other end of the spectrum, I perform these types of assessments with high achievers such as executives thinking of a career change, or athletes who are retiring from sport.

Sometimes people believe they are already on the right career path, but want to be sure. For example, I help people figure this out before making a big decision, such as whether to leave their corporate job and become an entrepreneur or go to medical school. These assessments help people figure out what career paths are suited to their Basic Personality Tendencies, values, passions, intellectual/cognitive abilities, and their other strengths and weaknesses.

One of the keys to these assessments is the measurement of vocational or career interests. Keep in mind that knowing your interests doesn't tell you whether you have the ability, skill, motivation, opportunities, education, or training background needed to succeed at a particular type of career. What it does shed light on is whether your interests in particular types of activities match those found in specific types of careers, or of people already in those types of careers. It tells you which types of careers or job-related activities you'll likely find most satisfying.

Undoubtedly, your values will also dictate what types of careers you will find most satisfying. So keep these in mind when examining your career choices.

I want to bring up a few connections between your career interests and your Basic Personality Tendencies.

Recall that there are 5 Basic Personality Tendencies that have been found across cultures. These include the following:

- Negative Emotions

- Extraversion

- Openness to Change/New Experiences

- Agreeableness

- Motivation/Self-Control

Working in a career that is not at all congruent with your personality is going to be the quickest road to unhappiness. For example, I've assessed hundreds of potential police recruits applying to work as police constables. Occasionally, I have come across those whose personalities are not well-suited for front-line police work.

I recall assessing one candidate who had one of the least suited personality profiles for front-line police work. First of all, he was quite high in Negative Emotions. As you can probably guess, policing can be pretty stressful work. If you have a hard time controlling your fear and anger, for example, you're going to have a hard time dealing with the stresses of the job.

The person was also very high on Openness. Police work is very structured, at times monotonous, with little wiggle room when it comes to the law. Those who are very high on Openness tend to be very open to different points of view and ways of doing things. Generally, a police officer requires more practical thinking with clear ideas of what is right and wrong.

And if these issues weren't enough, this person was also very high on Agreeableness. Recall that those who are very high on Agreeableness tend to be very trusting, honest, and sympathetic. These are not bad traits to have, but when dealing with criminals, you need a certain level of skepticism, guardedness, and tough-mindedness or else you'll probably be too nice to arrest anyone, even if they deserve it. At the same time, you can be too disagreeable, which can be even more damaging.

With this personality profile, the candidate would be very likely to be unhappy and out of their element most of the time in the field of law enforcement.

There are a number of Basic Personality Tendency profiles that can influence what types of career interests you are likely to have. Keep in mind that these are just tendencies and you shouldn't rule in or rule out a particular type of career solely based on these patterns. If you fall at the extremes in your ratings on the Basic Personality Tendency dimensions, then the career interest description is more likely to be accurate than if you fall somewhere in the middle.

Also keep in mind that you can work in almost any career regardless of your personality traits. Jobs and careers are multifaceted in terms of what you do during the workday. But there are certain types of jobs or certain job activities that your personality may make you more suited for.

NEGATIVE EMOTIONS & CAREERS

Generally, if you are high on Negative Emotions, then you're going to work best in career settings where there isn't a lot of stress. Prototypical careers would be a hairstylist, librarian, or a lab technician.

On the other hand, if you are very low on this dimension, then you will be more able to handle careers with high levels of stress without being overwhelmed. Surgeons, fighter pilots, and hostage negotiators would fall in this category.

EXTRAVERSION & CAREERS

If you are high on Extraversion, you'll probably enjoy careers that are fast-paced with a lot of social contact. Those high on this dimension feel at home in positions like sales, management, leadership, politics, teaching, event planning, nursing, and family medicine.

If you are also low in Agreeableness, then you may make a good leader given you are likely dominant and self-assured. You would enjoy making big decisions, and directing and managing others.

If you are low on Extraversion, you'll tend to feel most comfortable in positions where there is less stimulation, especially social stimulation. You will want to be in positions where there are large chunks of time where you can work alone or one-on-one, such as working as a librarian, bookkeeper, writer, or scientist.

OPENNESS & CAREERS

If you are high on Openness, you'll likely feel most attracted to careers that involve the appreciation of art or the use of your curiosity, creativity, vision, or other "outside-the-box" thinking. Prototypical examples include work as an artist, entrepreneur, designer, or visionary leader.

If you are low on Openness, you'll gravitate toward careers where you can use your practicality, logic, and clear ideas about how things should be done. Good examples of related careers are orthopedic surgery, technician, and quality control specialist.

AGREEABLENESS & CAREERS

If you are high on Agreeableness, you may enjoy careers where you're in a friendly environment and you can be helpful and cooperative. Good examples of suitable careers include working as a personal trainer, social worker, and a customer service representative.

If you also happen to be high on Motivation, then you're likely an ideal team player and highly valued in team contexts. You'll be willing to do the difficult, but thankless, tasks that need to be done to help the team.

If you are low on Agreeableness, you'll probably feel most comfortable in positions where being nice and friendly is not necessary. You'll work best when you can exercise your skepticism and competitive nature, and where you're free to speak your mind. Great examples of this are judges, criminal investigators, quality control specialists, forensic psychologists, and trial lawyers.

MOTIVATION & CAREERS

Lastly, if you are high on Motivation, you'll likely do well in any type of job you choose, as this dimension is the number one personality predictor of job success across industries.

But you may work best in careers where you can work hard and move up the ladder. You won't need much structure to keep you on track, as you have your own internal structure. You won't need a manager breathing down your neck to make sure you're doing your work. There are no real prototypical careers for those with high levels of Motivation, as this constellation of traits is helpful in almost any type of work.

If you are low on Motivation, however, you'll probably work best in environments with clear structure and rules for you to follow. Any job that has clear expectations and procedures will help keep you on track. Work on an assembly line, in the military, or even on professional sports teams are good examples of jobs with high levels of structure and organization.

If you happen to be low on Motivation and high on Openness, you're likely somewhat of a dreamer in that your mind may be less influenced and constrained by old ways of doing things or ambiguity. This is a great profile to have when it comes to brainstorming. You'll likely need people who are high on Motivation to carry your ideas through, as they are more methodical and organized.

EXTRAVERSION & OPENNESS PROFILES & CAREERS

When we look at other combinations of Basic Personality Tendencies, particularly those involving Openness and Extraversion, we can find even more specific types of career interests or activities that may be suitable.

If you are high on Openness and high on Extraversion, you are more likely to be interested in careers where there is a lot of change and where you can have a lot of different experiences you can share with others. You'll enjoy fast-paced and exciting careers where you can also engage your creativity. For example, you're likely to enjoy careers that involve public speaking, teaching others, or meeting people different from you.

If you are low on Openness and low on Extraversion, then you're going to feel most at home in careers where a large part of the work is done alone or one-on-one, and in a slower-paced environment. Working as a bookkeeper or accountant, technician, or technical writer are congruent with this personality profile.

If you are instead high on Openness and low on Extraversion, then you may feel most at home in activities where you get to introspect more, like painting and creative writing.

If you are low on Openness and high on Extraversion, then you're likely attracted to careers that involve mainstream ideas and products. Selling traditional and practical products like home improvement tools, cars, or financial products may interest you.

CAREER INTEREST INVENTORIES

One of the best ways to get an idea of your career interests is to take a reliable and well-validated career or vocational interest measure. Career or vocational interest inventories are psychological tests that call for you to respond in terms of your level of agreement with, or interest in, statements such as descriptions of work activities. Your responses are scored and compared to various groups. You are then provided with feedback about what types of career interests are dominant for you. Some measures even compare you to people already working in particular careers.

There are many vocational interest measures on the market. Most of the good ones require a visit to a counseling psychologist or career counselor. There also are many different ways to measure your interests. Some measures compare your responses to others who are in particular fields. Others look at your "work personality" and help you figure out whether your personality theoretically fits with specific career types, like the idea that Extraverts theoretically enjoy sales. Other measures look at how your interests theoretically match up with those in particular careers.

It can be really hard to decide which measure to take and even harder to find a qualified person to administer and interpret the measure you want.

WHAT TO LOOK FOR IN A CAREER INTEREST MEASURE

Ideally, a good career or vocational interest measure provides you with feedback on the following:

- How you compare to others, regardless of what career they are in, in terms of interests in performing specific activities. For example, a high score on a particular scale, like Performing Arts, would indicate that you show a preference for working in settings involving the activities described by the scale name, which in this case is enjoying performing for an audience. A low score would indicate that you would prefer not to work in such settings and would probably find this type of work unsatisfying.

- How you compare with others on broad patterns of interests rather than interests in specific activities. Many measures refer to these as "work personality." Popular themes include: *Expressive/Artistic, Logical/Practical/Realistic, Inquiring/Investigative, Social/Helping, Conventional, and Enterprising.*

- How your interests compare to university or college students of various majors. This is especially useful if you are open to retraining or are about to start post-secondary schooling.

- How your interests compare to the interests of people already successfully working in specific careers.

- Recommendations on how to further explore the career interests identified by the measure.

Thankfully, there is a high-quality measure available online for a relatively small fee that provides the feedback noted above. This is the Jackson Vocational Interest Survey, or JVIS.

The JVIS is arguably the best vocational interest inventory ever developed. It was devised by one of the world's foremost psychological test developers, Douglas Jackson. It was set up using the most advanced statistical methods for psychological tests. It also combines the strengths of many of the other measures available. You can take the test on-line here: http://FriesenPerformance.com.jvis.com/take

Something to keep in mind with the JVIS, or any measure for that matter, is that no measure is 100 percent accurate. Also, our interests can also change over time. And of course, you need to carefully consider many factors, including your Basic Personality Tendencies, values, purpose, skills, talents, weaknesses, educational background, work experience, and unique circumstances before making any career decisions.

You may also want to discuss your career interests test results and your plans with a counseling psychologist or career counselor. These professionals can help you interpret what the results mean if needed and help you figure out where to get additional educational and career information. Such professionals are often found in high schools, colleges, universities, private practices, and employment centers.

A GUIDED
CAREER-DISCOVERY EXERCISE

Another way to get in touch with your interests is to complete my Career Interests Guided Discovery Exercise below. This is a compilation of what I believe are the most powerful questions you can ask yourself to get in touch with your career passions and interests. There are no scoring keys or right or wrong answers.

This should be considered more of a process exercise. In others words, simply taking the time to think deeply about these questions will give you ideas, insights, and new perspectives on yourself and what you should be doing with your career.

Find a time and place where you can do this without interruption for at least 15 to 30 minutes. Turn off your phone, computer, TV, and put a Do Not Disturb sign on your door if you have to. Take 10 slow and long breaths as described in the Strengths Guided Discovery Exercise above. This should result in a mental state of calm focus and help clear your mind before you begin.

Go to FriesenPerformance.com/Achieve-Bonus-Materials to download a printable Career Interests Guided Discovery Exercise.

Academic Interests

1. Throughout your schooling, which classes/subjects did you enjoy the most or find most interesting?

_____

_____

_____

2. What was it about the classes/subjects you found interesting?

_____

_____

_____

3. Throughout your schooling, which classes/subjects were you interested in least or enjoyed the least?

_____

_____

_____

4. What was it about the classes/subjects you found uninteresting?

_____

_____

_____

Work Interests

1. Of all of the jobs you've had, which were your favorites?

_____

_____

_____

2. What was it about each job that you enjoyed?

_____

_____

_____

3. Of all of the jobs you've had, which were your least favorite?

_____

_____

_____

4. What was it about each job that you didn't enjoy?

_____

_____

_____

5. What type of work seems boring or tedious to you?

_____

_____

_____

6. What type of work seems interesting and exciting to you?

_____

_____

_____

Hobbies

1. What sorts of activities or hobbies did you especially enjoy as a child or teenager?

_____

_____

_____

2. What sorts of activities or hobbies did you especially enjoy as an adult?

_____

_____

_____

3. List your top three favorite television shows of all time: For each show, what was it about the show that you found appealing? Can you see any commonalities among the shows?

_____

_____

_____

_____

_____

4. List your top three favorite movies: For each movie, what was it about the movie that you found appealing? Can you see any commonalities among the movies?

_____

_____

_____

_____

_____

5. List your top three favorite fiction books: For each book, what was it about the book that you found appealing? Can you see any commonalities among the books?

_____

_____

_____

_____

_____

6. List your top three favorite nonfiction books: For each book, what was it about the book that you found appealing? Can you see any commonalities among the books?

_____

_____

_____

_____

_____

_____

7. Are there any characters from any of the above who inspired you or who you admired?

_____

_____

Passions

1. Who in your life inspires you or who do you look up to?

_____

_____

2. What was/is it about this person that you admire?

_____

_____

_____

3. What makes you feel passion or excitement?

_____

_____

_____

Dreams

1. If you didn't have to worry about making a living or what others thought of you, what would you do with your time?

_____

_____

_____

2. What are you most drawn to doing? Forget prestige, your friends' ideas, your parents' goals for you, and money.

_____

_____

_____

3. What would be your top three dream jobs if money were no object?

_____

_____

_____

4. Can you see any commonalities between your top three dream jobs?

_____

_____

_____

5. What do you see as the main barriers to obtaining your top three dream jobs?

_____

_____

_____

Once you've done this exercise, ask yourself:

- What did I learn about myself and my interests?

- Is there any way to tie in the interests I discovered in this process with what I am currently doing as a career?

- Is there any way to tie in the interests I discovered in this process with what I can do as a future career?

- Is there some action I can take to look into the possibility of incorporating my interests into my current career or another career?

Now put your responses away for at least a full day. After a day or two, come back to what you wrote and follow the breathing instructions noted above. Review what you've written and see what kind of reactions you get when you read it for the second time. Note any new insights or ideas.

Now that you have a better understanding of your basic personality, values, strengths, talents, skills, and interests, it's time to put it all together to figure out your purpose or mission.

Resources

How to do What You Love by Paul Graham:
http://FriesenPerformance.com.paulgraham.com/love.html
How to Find Fulfilling Work by Roman Krznaric:
http://amzn.com/1250030692
Finding Your Element by Ken Robinson: http://amzn.com/0143125516
Jackson Vocational Interest Survey (JVIS): You can take the test on-line here: http://FriesenPerformance.com.jvis.com/take/

BONUS MATERIAL

Visit FriesenPerformance.com/Achieve-Bonus-Materials to download printable copies of both the Strengths Guided Discovery Exercise AND Career Interests Guided Discovery Exercise.

STEP 4

KNOW YOUR 'WHY'

Chapter 12

KNOW YOUR PURPOSE OR MISSION

Efforts and courage are not enough without purpose and direction.
— John F. Kennedy

Definiteness of purpose is the starting point of all achievement.
— W. Clement Stone

Think about the people our society admires for the great things they have done. Think of Martin Luther King Jr., Steve Jobs, Mahatma Gandhi, Albert Einstein, Jackie Robinson, Marie Curie, Oskar Schindler, Michael Jordan, George Washington, Louise Pasteur, Muhammad Ali, Wolfgang Amadeus Mozart, Rosa Parks, Galileo Galelei, Nelson Mandela, and Mother Teresa.

These people knew who they were, what they valued, what they were good at, and what moved them.

But they had something more than that. They had figured out their purpose or mission. Their purpose for being on this earth. They realized their life had a meaning that was bigger than themselves. Some of them paid dearly for pursuing their path. Some even paid with their life. But I doubt any of them would have had it any other way.

I don't believe you can really figure out your life's meaning, purpose, or mission without developing an intimate knowledge of yourself. This book is designed to provide you with that knowledge. This is not to say that your purpose or mission won't change over time, or that you only have one purpose or mission. But having purposes or missions that are bigger than yourself will make you unstoppable.

You may be a professional athlete and playing your sport is in line with your personality, values, strengths, and interests. But your mission or purpose may not be simply to "play tennis." It may be bigger than that.

Your tennis career may also be about your kids. Maybe you want to give them the financial freedom you never had growing up. Maybe you want to show them that they too can achieve their goals and dreams if they work hard enough. Maybe you want to be a role model for them by showing them how to live a life driven by the right values.

Or maybe it's all of these things. Each person's purpose and mission is unique to them. Nobody can tell you what it is.

THERE IS A COST ASSOCIATED WITH YOUR CHOICES

I want to make a few things clear here. Doing the exercises in this book will help you better understand and motivate yourself, and make sure you are pursuing and achieving goals that are in line with what you are, what you value, what you are interested in, and your purpose or mission. In other words, knowing the WHAT, WHY, and HOW. This is the path to achieving great things in your life. At the same time, you may have noticed that the steps to achieving are not easy or simple.

But the reality is that you are going to face pain and setbacks no matter which path you choose. All choices in life open some doors and close others. With each choice there is good and bad. Each choice comes at a cost. To be the world's best mixed martial artist or be one of the country's top business consultants, there is going to be a cost, even if only temporary.

Even if you make the best choice for you, realize and accept that it will still be a struggle. You need to be ready for this and be willing to accept it as par for the course. Keep in mind that even if you complete all the exercises in this book and find your dream job or reach your goal, there will still be parts of it that you don't like or that are hard or make you uncomfortable.

The idea that you're going to achieve your goals or find out exactly what you love to do — and then love every second of it — is a myth. Don't get me wrong. I'm not suggesting you live your life as a martyr. Following the strategies in this series of books will reduce the amount of suffering you experience in your life. But nothing worth achieving comes without a struggle.

Understand that there's a difference between suffering and struggling. As the Dalai Lama wrote: "Pain is inevitable. Suffering is optional." So you will struggle and feel pain. Whether you suffer depends on how you see it. If you live your life and pursue goals that are in line with who you are, what you value, and your purpose or mission, then the struggle will be worth it.

So make no mistake, you will face self-doubt, uncertainty, mental and physical pain, and failure when pursuing your goals. These are the rules of the game. You need to make sure you're working on goals worth the inevitable struggle that will come as you pursue them.

The best way to reduce the amount of suffering is to determine and then follow your purpose and mission. You'll also have to find a way to love the process, the journey. If not, it won't be worth it. One way to make sure your journey is fulfilling is to make sure you're living your life congruent with your personality, deepest values, strengths, passions, and mission.

There is a cost to every choice we make. Understand and accept this fact and you will go far. Hoping you won't feel pain along the way will only lead to disappointment. Even success, happiness, and living fully comes with a price. Life is difficult. Accept it and keep moving forward.

THE CASE OF VIKTOR FRANKL

Ever more people today have the means to live, but no meaning to live for.
— Viktor Frankl

Everyone has his own specific vocation or mission in life to carry out a concrete assignment which demands fulfillment. Therein he cannot be replaced, nor can his life be repeated. Thus, everyone's task is as unique as is his specific opportunity to implement it.
— Viktor Frankl

One of the best examples of living a meaningful life that was in line with one's values and mission is the life and work of Dr. Viktor Frankl. If you're not familiar with Frankl, I highly recommend you Google him. His story is both horrifying and inspiring.

Frankl was a Jewish psychiatrist and neurologist living in Austria when the Nazis took power. Frankl's story highlights my earlier point about how each choice we make has benefits and consequences that we have to accept responsibility for.

During the Nazi's reign, despite the persecution of Jews, Frankl made a choice to stay in Nazi-occupied Austria. He was well aware of the risks he was taking. He even had his own immigration visa to the United States, but decided against leaving. He did so for two reasons. One was that his parents didn't have visas and he didn't want to desert them. Secondly, he was the director of neurology in a hospital for mentally ill Jewish patients and felt a strong sense of moral responsibility to protect them from the Nazis.

Despite the danger to his own life, he felt his purpose at that time was to sabotage Nazi procedures by making false diagnoses to prevent the euthanasia of his patients. In other words, he made a choice and was fully aware of the consequences of his choice. He decided to live true to his values and purpose and not let circumstances or his fear dictate his choices. Unfortunately, he paid a price for this.

Frankl and his family were sent to Nazi concentration camps. While a prisoner in the camps, Frankl observed his fellow captives and discovered that, despite facing the same horrific conditions, including diseases and starvation, there appeared to be systematic differences between those who lived and died of natural causes that were in line with his previous ideas of the importance of finding meaning in life. His observations lead him to conclude that those who lived and those who died differed in their perception of the meaning, purpose, and mission they had for living.

In his book, *Man's Search for Meaning*, he notes: "Everything can be taken from a man but one thing ... the last of the human freedoms ... to choose one's attitude in any given set of circumstances, to choose one's own way."

This became all too apparent to Frankl when he was being tortured by his Nazi captors. He realized the Nazis could do whatever they wanted to his body, but they couldn't destroy his mind unless he let them. In the camps, he knew he had to survive to spread his message to the world. This sense of meaning and purpose is what kept him alive.

Amazingly, Frankl survived three years in multiple Nazi concentration camps. When he was finally released, he officially learned that most of his family, including his parents, his brother, and even his pregnant wife, had died or were murdered in the camps. Although he felt unbelievable despair, he found purpose in further spreading his message about the importance of finding meaning and purpose in one's life, and other observations about human nature he obtained through his experience in the concentration camps. Within a year of his release, he wrote *Man's Search for Meaning*, a book that has now sold over 10 million copies around the world.

Thankfully, we don't have to go through what Frankl did to learn this lesson. We do need to be thankful to people like Frankl and others who have shown us just how powerful it can be when we live a life congruent with our values and with a purpose bigger than ourselves.

THE CASE OF JANET

When I first met Janet, she looked like she had it all. She dressed impeccably, drove a Mercedes-Benz, and was tall and attractive. When she spoke, she commanded herself with authority. It was also quickly apparent that she was as smart as they come. She displayed all the characteristics of what it would take to become a high-powered lawyer.

Janet was a highly paid personal injury lawyer working her way up in a prestigious law firm that primarily defended institutions being sued by injured employees. She came to me because she saw herself as a high achiever and wanted help taking her performance and productivity to the next level in order to reach her goal of becoming a partner in the firm.

I don't always start off with the exercises in this book with all of my clients. But despite Janet's outward appearance and persona, something seemed off about her. I had the suspicion that she was not feeling fulfilled. Because of this, I recommended we start with some of the exercises from this book before pursuing her original goal of learning strategies to maximize her daily performance.

At first, she was resistant to the idea of doing these exercises. She even made a joking comment that it was a little more "shrink-like" than she expected from me. At first she commented that it would be a waste of time and that if we did it at all, that we should do it in a few months. I told her we could, but that I had an inclination that this would be helpful for her. She grudgingly agreed.

At our third meeting, we did the Funeral Exercise. For the first time, she looked uncomfortable and less confident. Once we began the Values Survey though, she broke down and sobbed.

She relayed that deep down she must have always known that being a lawyer was not her real calling. She recalled that her parents never directly told her she should apply to law school, but they had high expectations of her and expected she train in some sort of profession that required higher education. She relayed how she was continuously reinforced by external forces like praise from her parents, professors, and peers. She recalled people telling her in law school that she was going to be one of the top lawyers in the area. This kept her going.

Janet also felt she had to be continuously doing something productive, a problem common to those high on the personality tendency of Motivation like Janet. If she ever slowed down or took time off, she would feel a little depressed and down.

After a few sessions, she admitted that her dogged pursuit of her goal of becoming a partner in the firm was destroying her health, friendships, and family. Her pursuit became all-consuming and she felt endless pressure to perform. As we worked through this, Janet came to realize that she was not living in line with what was truly important to her. She was living incongruent with some of her core values. Janet realized that her purpose was not to work in the personal injury arena.

We worked together for a number of months. We did a number of the other strategies outlined in this book to help her learn more about her personality, values and purpose, and to develop goals that were in line with these. She found a new purpose and mission that included more than her career.

Janet ended up changing the type of law she practiced. She now works in healthcare law. She changed her life mission from being the best personal injury lawyer in the area to being a great lawyer — but also to being the best mother and wife she can be. She realized that her health was important for all aspects of her life mission and began to prioritize this as well. She is still driven to do well, but works fewer hours. She finds she has more time to spend with her family, friends, and even herself. She reports she's never been happier and has no regrets changing the focus of her career.

THE DEATHBED LITERATURE

I want to point out here that Janet's discoveries are in line with what is known as the "deathbed literature." A famous example of this is the work of

Australian palliative care nurse Bronnie Ware.[39] Ware recorded the epiphanies, regrets, and wishes of her dying patients. She found that those who were dying generally reported wishing they:

- Lived their lives being more true to themselves and not by others' or society's expectations. This included following their own dreams and passions.

- Took advantage of their lives more when they were healthy.

- Didn't work so long and hard at the expense of their other roles.

- Expressed to others how they truly felt about things.

- Stayed in touch with friends.

- Got out of old patterns of thinking and behaving that prevented them from making the choice to be happy.

We can learn a lot about living a life with meaning from the dying. Please don't wait until that point to make the right choices. Janet is sure glad she didn't.

JANET'S CASE AND HAPPINESS RESEARCH

Janet's case also highlights the research on happiness.[40] I brought this up earlier in this book, but feel it's worth repeating here. Seligman and others have found that what should be considered as happiness is really a combination of a number of factors. These factors make up the acronym P.E.R.M.A. For your review, these include the following:

---

[39] Ware (2012). The Top Five Regrets of the Dying: A Life Transformed by the Dearly Departing: http://goo.gl/RZjOhD

[40] Seligman (2004). Authentic Happiness: Using the New Positive Psychology to Realize Your Potential for Lasting Fulfillment: http://goo.gl/0TQ8hS

- **Positive Emotions:** Experiencing and focusing on positive emotions and having a realistic-to-optimistic outlook.

- **Engagement:** Being engaged in and absorbed by activities.

- **Relationships:** Social connection and positive relationships are essential for wellbeing.

- **Meaning:** Living your life with a sense of purpose and meaning. This includes living your life in line with your values, purpose, and mission.

- **Accomplishment:** Making and achieving even small goals.

Janet not only changed the focus of her career, she changed her life. Of course, her personality didn't change. She continued to be high on Motivation in that she continued to be hard-working, motivated, and achievement-oriented. But now these traits were focused on more than just her work.

She channeled her strength of Motivation into being the best she could be in the areas of positive emotions, being fully engaged and present in whatever she was doing, nurturing relationships, focusing on meaning with her family, friends, and career, and accomplishing her goals. She also tapped into her deeper values and searched long and hard to figure out what was truly important to her and what her life's mission was.

HOW TO USE THIS IN YOUR LIFE

Many of us live our lives chasing fame, fortune, and thrills, only to end up chronically dissatisfied by these pursuits. There is nothing wrong with these pursuits per se, but they are often pursued for external reasons, such as cultural pressures and values espoused by the media and their coverage of the celebrity lifestyle.

You will never be truly satisfied when your values and purpose come from outside of you. They need to come from within you. Remember, there is nothing worse in life than living with regret. Choose your purpose wisely!

Taking everything you've learned about yourself in this process, do your best to answer the following questions:

- What do you really want out of life?

- What do you want your life to stand for?

- What sort of person do you want to be?

- What do you want to do with your life?

- What do you believe your purpose(s) or mission(s) is (are) in this life?

- What were you uniquely put on this earth to achieve?

Now put this into a paragraph and fine-tune it. You now have your living purpose or mission document to guide your decision-making through your life.

CONCLUSION

At this point, you should have a better understanding of your Basic Personality Tendencies. You've also gotten in touch with what is truly important to you. You know your interests, passions, strengths, talents, and skills. You have a better idea what your purpose or mission is.

Your next step is to translate this into concrete goals to achieve.

BONUS MATERIAL
Visit FriesenPerformance.com/Achieve-Bonus-Materials to download a printable poster with the quotes found in this chapter AND the Purpose/Mission Exercise Worksheet.

STEP 5

KNOW YOUR GOALS

Chapter 13

CHOOSE GOALS THAT ARE RIGHT FOR YOU

A goal is a dream with a deadline.
— Napoleon Hill

Goal-setting is powerful because it provides focus. It gives us the ability to hone in on the exact actions we need to perform to achieve everything we desire in life.
— Jim Rohn

Now that you have a better idea of your basic personality, have gotten in touch with what's truly important to you, understand what your strengths, passions, and interests are, and have a living purpose or mission document, we have to translate this into a vision and road map for the future.

For some of you, the exercises you've done so far in this book may have confirmed what you already knew. If so, that's great. These exercises help to give us perspective to make sure we are on the right track. Now you know you are and can be confident as you move forward.

For others, it may have helped you realize that you were focusing on the wrong things. Maybe you realized that you were living your life based on other peoples' dreams, expectations, and agendas. Maybe you were working really hard on moving up the corporate ladder only to realize that what the corporation stands for and the type of person you have become or have to become, is not in line with what really matters most to you or what you're passionate about.

If this is you, then you really need to think long and hard about what your next steps should be. You may decide that you should stay on your current path given your unique circumstances. Or maybe you decide to make a major change. Either way, these exercises should prevent you from living your life blind to what you really want and what you should be doing. I don't believe that 'ignorance is bliss'. I think ignorance is ignorance.

The previous exercises and the exercises in this chapter will help you see that happiness is less about the end result, and more about living your life congruent with your personality, values, and what you're really passionate about. In other words, you need to love the process — what it's going to take to reach your big goals — in order to truly succeed.

You may think you want the glory and the recognition that comes with winning a gold medal or becoming partner at your firm. You should really be asking yourself less about how great this would be, and more about whether you love the process, the lifestyle, and the day-to-day reality that will be required to reach your goal. You at least have to truly believe that achieving the goal is really worth all the work and sacrifice it will require. Then you can decide whether it's worth it for you. Otherwise, you won't have the stamina and drive to do what it takes day-in and day-out.

Maybe you fantasize about being a writer. Unless you love the daily grind of writing when you don't feel inspired, are ready and willing to accept rejection by publishers and being criticized by reviewers, and are willing to put in long and potentially lonely hours slogging away at your computer, becoming a writer is not the right path for you.

This happens to us more often than not. We fall in love with the idea of something or the outcome, but we don't step back and really think about whether the daily activities and sacrifices we will have to make are in line with our personalities, values, passions, interests, and strengths. So think about the goal itself, but think a whole lot more about the lifestyle it will require to achieve the goal.

As I noted earlier, you can think of your personality, values, and passions as needs. You need to have them met on a daily or weekly basis or else you're not going to feel satisfied. So you need to make sure that the goals you set are in line with your personality, values, passions, and purpose or mission. This is the key to greatness and to happiness.

Once you understand this, you will see that there are many paths you can take to satisfy these needs. Your original goal may be one of many options. So you may have a goal to earn a million dollars by a certain date. It may be that what you really want is respect or freedom, and it's really not about the money in the first place. So feel free to keep the million-dollar goal as long as you know why you really want it.

Or maybe there are other things you can do to get respect and freedom, like publishing a book that people find helpful and respect you for. The lifestyle of a writer may also fulfill that need for more freedom in your life, especially relative to your corporate job. So think more about who you are and what is most important to you when setting your goals later in this chapter.

Also remember that the exercises in the previous chapters are not something you do once and then forget about. You need to continually be real with yourself. You need to check-in. Things change. What we value changes. Our missions change as we learn new things, develop new skills, and with time. Our interests change too.

So you should consider doing the Funeral Exercise, Values Survey, and even the exercises in the Know Your Talents, Skills, & Interests and Know Your Purpose or Mission chapters about once a year to make sure you continue focusing on the right things.

I think we all know what goals are. But to make sure we are on the same page, goals can be generally defined as achieving some standard or result.

The general process of setting and achieving goals is relatively straightforward. The first step involves deciding on a goal and then vividly imagining yourself accomplishing that goal. Then you need to work backwards to figure out what steps you need to take to bring you from where you are now to where you want to be.

Before we get into the process of setting goals properly, there are a number of things about goals that will help you better understand them.

How Your Basic Personality Shapes Goals

It's great to know your personality, what's truly important to you, your interests, strengths, and even your purpose or mission. But we need to translate all of this into actual goals. To do this, we need to start with the long view and work our way back. Before we do this, review your Basic Personality Tendency results. Knowing your personality will give you an advantage when it comes to figuring out what motivates you when pursuing your goals.

At this point, you're probably not surprised to hear that your Basic Personality Tendencies can have an effect on how you approach goals and even whether you set goals in the first place.

Not surprisingly, those of you who are high on Motivation can easily and readily set and achieve goals. Be forewarned though, you may be prone to setting and working hard on the wrong goals at times, due to having difficulties seeing the bigger picture as noted previously.

If you also happen to be high on Extraversion, then you likely pursue your goals with energy and enthusiasm. If you're high on Motivation and low on Extraversion, then you may also work hard toward your goals but at a slower and possibly less contagiously enthusiastic manner.

As noted earlier in this book, if you are low on Negative Emotions and high on Motivation, your personality is tailor-made for high achievement because you're probably good at setting and achieving goals and don't get too worked-up by the stresses and failures you'll face.

But if you are high on Negative Emotions and Motivation you are at risk for failure when it comes to achieving big and ambitious goals because you'll have a hard time dealing with the inevitable stress and setback. This can lead to burnout.

Those of you who are very low on Motivation probably set very few goals. You have a hard time sticking to the plans you've set out. If you happen to also be high on Extraversion, you're probably full of positive energy and enjoy thrills and adventures, but find it hard to channel your energy into goals and plans. And remember, that's ok. We are what we are. If you're fine with this, then all is good. But if you're unhappy about it, you can work to change it.

If you are low on Motivation and low on Extraversion, you may have a more lethargic style in that you take your time, don't feel rushed, and are not too concerned about setting and working toward big goals. You're probably satisfied taking a back seat and watching others do their thing.

Those low on Motivation and high on Negative Emotions face low odds of becoming a high achiever or reaching big and ambitious goals. To set and achieve big goals, you at least need motivation and drive. However, having this personality profile does not rule out being a high achiever. You will just have to have a very clear and strong passion, mission, and purpose, and then work very hard to tolerate, control, and harness your negative emotions.

ARE YOU ON OFFENSE OR DEFENSE?

Where you fall on the Negative Emotions continuum can influence the types of goals you set for yourself. Those susceptible to negative emotions and stress likely tend to focus on what Columbia University psychologist Heidi Halvorson calls prevention goals.

Being high on Negative Emotions can be thought of as being sensitive to punishment. In other words, you are not big on taking risks. Your goals and a lot of your decisions are likely based on preventing negative things from happening.

In sports, you may focus more on trying not to lose by playing defensively, rather than trying to win by taking big chances. This can lead you to never taking any big chances, and setting goals that are too safe. Big achievements will rarely occur with this type of prevention focus.

If you are high on Negative Emotions, you'll be able to motivate yourself by imagining all the negative things that will follow if you don't reach a goal or take an action. Maybe you have a steady but unfulfilling government job, but your real dream is to start your own consulting business. Thinking of all negative consequences of not starting your consulting business may motivate you effectively. So think of all of the pain you'll experience if you stay in your job, such as the regret of not pursuing your dream, feeling trapped, or the disappointment of your family and friends when you fail to follow your dreams.

Or maybe you have one more shot at making the Olympic team given your age, but are afraid to try and fail. Thinking of the negative consequences of not going for it will likely motivate you. So train yourself to think of all of the pain and regret you'll experience if you don't try, or the fact that your family and friends may be disappointed in you for not following your dreams.

On the other hand, if you are low on Negative Emotions, this too will likely shape the types of goals you'll make. Armed with this knowledge about yourself, you can learn the trick to motivate yourself.

If you are low on this dimension and high on Extraversion, you'll tend to have more of what Halvorson calls promotion-focused goals. This personality profile can be thought of as being sensitive to rewards and insensitive to punishment.

This means you're more likely to take risks and not sweat the small stuff. Coming up with big goals with the possibility of big payoffs is easy and motivating for you. The one drawback is that you may underestimate the risks and all the hard work involved in achieving your goal. So keep this in mind when setting your goals.

If you're low on Negative Emotions and high on Extraversion you'll be more likely to be motivated by thinking of all the positive things or gains from taking action and achieving your goal.

Using the same example that I used earlier in which you have a safe but unfulfilling government job but dream of having your own consulting business, you will be more motivated by thinking of all the benefits of leaving your current job to follow your passion. You can imagine all the pleasure and fulfillment you'll experience, such as the freedom, potential for increased pay, or how you'll impress your family and friends with your courage.

Or if you have one last shot at making the Olympic team, you'll be more motivated by thinking of all the benefits that come with the accomplishment. So think of the sense of accomplishment you'll experience by doing so. You can also think of the glory you'll experience if you go for it and make it and how proud your family and friends will be.

So knowing yourself is important. If you know – and accept – that you are high or low on Negative Emotions or Extraversion, you can learn to use it as a lever to help you achieve your goals.

UNDERSTANDING GOAL TYPES

There are two types of goals that we need to clarify — outcome and process goals. Success depends on having both types of goals clearly articulated in your mind and on paper.

Outcome goals are things you want to achieve and milestones you want to hit. This could be winning your division in your sport, getting drafted, or having your new product hit the top 100 in Amazon sales rankings in a specific category. Outcome goals are essential to achieving your potential. They give you something specific to aim for. They help motivate you.

But you can't stop at outcome goals. When you only have outcome goals, your day-to-day focus tends to be on these, which is referred to as having an outcome focus. Don't get me wrong, having an outcome focus is important at times, such as when you need to motivate yourself. But when you're trying to perform in competition or complete a difficult task, you typically don't want to be overly-focused on the outcome. If you overly focus on the outcome, you're likely to under-perform with the task at hand.

For example, I once worked with Joanna, an elite swimmer who came to see me because of chronic under-performance over two seasons. Joanna was primarily competing in the 1500 meter women's freestyle events. After a few weeks of working together, it became glaringly apparent what the problem was. Joanna's mind was stuck on outcome goals and focus.

Joanna had no problems articulating what her outcome goals were. She wanted to win each heat, be the best in her division, achieve a specific time in her races, and make the Olympic team. These are great outcome goals. They really helped motivate her when she had to get up at 5:30 a.m. to get to the pool to train. Whenever she wanted to push the snooze button, she reminded herself of her outcome goals and this propelled her out of bed.

The problem came when Joanna was competing. Based on bad advice from a previous mental skills coach, she focused exclusively on her outcome goals. She would visualize herself achieving these goals just prior to each race in the belief that this would raise her confidence and that high confidence was the key. In fact, Joanna had no problems with her confidence until she started focusing too much on her outcome goals during competition.

During the actual heats, she would also focus on her outcome goals. Based on the advice from her former mental skills coach, she repeatedly used the cue word "win." In other words, as she was swimming, in her mind she would repeat to herself "win...win...win..." and see herself winning in her mind's eye.

The problem is that this strategy is not in line with how the brain works. Our brains have limited attentional resources and focusing on the outcome of winning takes a lot of brain power. When this happens, there is much less power left over to focus on WHAT has to be done to actually win. I'm not saying that one should never focus on the outcome when in the middle of a performance. This can be helpful when you need a boost of adrenaline and energy as it can be highly motivating.

But when you focus exclusively on outcomes, you are pretty much guaranteed to underperform. Your brain needs help to stay focused on what it is supposed to focus on, like maintaining form. It needs to be reminded and be told what to do RIGHT NOW! Turns out, you can't actually fully control the outcome. That depends on a number of factors that you can't completely control. It could just turn out that the world's best 1500 meter swimmer decided she was going to be competing with you on this day, and so your probability of winning got a little smaller.

Also, as soon as your brain gets feedback that your goal of winning is not guaranteed, like when Joanna fell behind the pack, it tends to do one of two things. It puts you into a panic, which only makes you waste valuable energy and underperform even further. Or it tells you that your goal of winning is probably not going to happen so you might as well give up.

Our brains are really good at thinking in black-or-white or all-or-nothing terms. We've all seen this happen in sports and in our own lives. When we focus on outcome goals at the wrong times, we underperform. What we need is highly articulated and specific processes to focus on.

That's why process goals are essential. Process goals are things you are going to do on a week-to-week, day-to-day, minute-to-minute, and even second-to-second basis to get you to your outcome goals, or to help you live in line with your values. Process goals are the exact things you need to do or focus on at a particular time, or how you want to think and act based on your values.

For example, if your outcome goal is to write a book, then a process goal could be to write for three hours every day. You may also value authenticity and being real in your interactions with the world. So you may also have a process goal of "letting my true voice come through" when you write every day.

If your outcome goal is to master a particular skill or subject area, your process goal could be to practice that skill or read about that subject three times a week for 60 minutes each. You see how this is specific and instructional? Our brains can get easily overwhelmed and stressed when we over-focus on the longer-term outcome like making the Olympic team or publishing a book. We need to provide our brains with very specific information as to what to do and when to do it.

Our brains also like it better if we tell it what we should be doing as opposed to what we shouldn't be doing. So if your goal is to write a book in six months, then your process goals should **not** be "Don't waste time watching TV and surfing the Internet." Telling yourself not to do something or not to think about something usually only makes your impulse to do it stronger, or causes your mind to become fixated on it.

For example, one of the most debilitating Anxiety Disorders is Obsessive-Compulsive Disorder, or OCD. OCD is characterized by having unwanted thoughts, impulses, or images pop into mind, which often lead to compulsions to perform a behavior to reduce the anxiety associated with the unwanted mental events. Although OCD is a complicated disorder, one thing that can happen is sufferers have an unwanted thought.

For example, one of my former patients who lived on the 10th floor of a condominium building repeatedly had the thought "what if I lost it and jumped off the balcony!" The patient became fixated on the fact that they had such a terrible thought. Patients then do their damnedest to suppress the thought and even start avoiding situations that may trigger the thought. In this case, my patient started avoiding her balcony altogether.

But this ends up having the opposite effect by making the thought come back stronger and more frequently. The reality is having such thoughts is pretty common in people without OCD. But the act of trying to suppress the thoughts makes them stronger. For most of us, when we have such a thought we think it's odd, but then realize that our minds are just weird like that and we move on and forget about it. So telling yourself not to do something or not to think of something usually has the opposite effect.

So instead of setting process goals such as "Don't waste time watching TV and surfing the Internet", your goal should be: "Write for three hours each day." Or if you are a hockey player who gets checked off the puck in the corners because you tend to keep your head down, you should NOT tell yourself "don't keep my head down." You should tell yourself "Keep my head up!" Our brains like to have simple instructions as to what we should do, not what we should not do.

In Joanna's case, instead of focusing on her outcome goal of winning, I helped her develop process goals and focus. Joanna came up with simple instructions that she went over with herself before and during the races. During the races she shortened these instructions down to single cue-words such as "pace" to remind her to pace herself and conserve energy over the long race or "left...right...left...right..." to help focus her brain on the technique of the front crawl.

Without outcome goals, you will be aimless and paralyzed. Without process goals, you will have no plan of action to achieve your outcome goals. I can't emphasize this enough. You need to clearly articulate both types of goals if you are going to succeed.

SMART GOALS

Talking about SMART goals is getting a little cliché. But there is a reason why SMART goals won't go away. It's because setting goals that are not SMART is simply stupid.

Keep in mind that some of our goals are more expressions of our values or how we want to conduct ourselves. Although these are harder to quantify, you can usually still break them down into SMART goals.

While different authors have slightly different ways of defining some of the aspects of SMART goals, below is what I believe are the basic key factors in setting goals. SMART is an acronym for:

- Specific

- Measurable

- Achievable

- Relevant

- Time-Bound

So let's go into each one in more detail.

Specific: The goals you set should not be vague. They need to be specific. A vague goal would be: "Be the best wrestler I can be." A specific outcome goal would be: "Place #1 in my division." A specific process goal would be: "Run for 45 minutes every morning."

Measurable: You need a way to know whether your goal has been met. To do this, you need it to be measurable. The above outcome goal of "Place #1 in my division" is measurable, because, if you end up fourth, you know you didn't reach your goal. Similarly, the process goal of "Run for 45 minutes every morning" is easily measurable. If you only ran twice this week, you know you didn't achieve your goal. Making your goals measurable ensures you've specified exactly what you want.

Achievable: This is where you get real with yourself. I'm all for dreaming up big goals, but I'm not into setting people up for failure. If you've invested years of training but still can't sing worth a dime, a goal of becoming an opera singer is not achievable. Or if you have a record of 0 wins and 27 loses in your wrestling division, having the goal of placing #1 in your division in a few months is probably not realistic or achievable and will set you up for failure. Having the outcome goal or "Winning at least twice this season" is much more achievable. So make sure you set big and ambitious goals that are still achievable.

Relevant: Your goals should be in line with your personality, values, strengths, interests, passions, and purpose. They need to be relevant to you, and what's important to you. The exercises in the previous chapters helped you determine whether the goals you set for yourself are relevant and important to you.

Time-bound: As Milton Erickson noted, "A goal without a date is just a dream." Giving yourself a deadline is essential. If your goal is to "Place #1 in my division" you should add a deadline. So it would be better to say: "Place #1 in my division by the end of next season." Having a deadline will provide you with a sense of urgency and propel you into action. If you keep making goals without a deadline, your chances of achieving them is greatly reduced.

So when setting your goals later in this chapter, make sure they are SMART goals!

HOW TO PICK YOUR TARGETS

A goal without a plan is just a wish.
—Antoine de Saint-Exupery

If you've been doing the exercises outlined so far in this book, you're ready for goal setting. Remember Napoleon Hill's quote at the beginning of this chapter, "A goal is a dream with a deadline." This is where you turn your dreams into a plan of action.

But also remember what you learned about yourself throughout this book. You want your goals to be in line with your Basic Personality Tendencies, values, strengths, passions, and mission or purpose. In other words, you want to make sure you set the right goals for you.

The first step is to decide on some long-term goals and then work your way back. You then set medium-term goals, such as 10-year goals, and then work your way back to 5-year, 1-year, 6-month, 1-month, 1-week, and then even daily goals. This is not an easy task, but is the best way to take yourself from where you are now to where you want to be.

Also, make your goals as SMART as possible. They should be Specific, Measurable, Achievable, Relevant, and Time-Bound. You'll notice, however, that it is much harder to meet all the criteria for SMART goals when setting your long-term goals.

You may notice that there is a blending of your values, mission, and purpose with your long-term goals. Sometimes our goals are more expressions of our values or how we want to live, and these are harder to quantify using the SMART method. That's ok. Your goals will become SMART-er as you work your way backwards.

Without setting goals, life will set them for you. So if you want to steer your own ship, you need to decide which goals you are willing to commit to and then take consistent action to bring yourself closer to them. Tony Robbins said it best: "The path to success is to take massive, determined action."

At the same time, your goals are not set in stone. Both your outcome and process goals can change over time and that is why you will review them regularly. Some of your process goals may need to be repeatedly tweaked to make sure they are bringing you closer to achieving your outcome goals. To quote Tony Robbins again: "If you do what you've always done, you'll get what you've always gotten."

IDENTIFYING YOUR DESTINATION

Now you are going to figure out what your long-term goals are. And I really mean long-term here. For this exercise, I want you to think about what you want to achieve by the time you retire in the main areas of your life that are important to you.

You may have noticed that some of the categories provided below may not seem all that important to you at this point in your life. But believe me, when you retire, you better hope that you took most of these areas pretty seriously. You may also have additional areas of your life that are important to you that are not listed below. You can put these under Other Goals.

For each of the categories, I want you to think of at least two outcome goals with at least one process goal for each outcome goal

Remember, outcome goals are the things you want to achieve, or milestones you want to hit, that give you something specific to target. Process goals are things you're going to do on a regular basis to get you to your outcome goals, or help you live in line with your values. So make sure your process goals complement your outcome goals.

Also, when you write down your goals, put them in the present tense and in the first person. In other words, write them as if they are happening right now. For some of the long-term goals, you can use past tense as you will see in the example below. But do your best to keep them in the present tense. There is some research that suggests writing out your goals this way is more effective.

Also, each goal should be stated in terms of what you want to achieve, not what you don't want to achieve. So instead of stating a goal like this — "I am NOT sick and crippled" — you should write "I am as healthy and fit as possible."

Below is an example of the long-term outcome and process goals of a young entrepreneur client of mine for illustrative purposes. Like all of the examples in this book, the name and details have been altered to protect her anonymity.

Sonia's Long-Term/Retirement Goals

Family Goals:

Outcome Goals:

1. I have happy and healthy children and grandchildren.

   #### Process Goals:

   I'm a loving mother and grandmother that is there for my children and grandchildren emotionally, physically, and financially.

2. I have a happy and fun-loving family.

   #### Process Goals:

   I am putting my family first.

   I try my best to make my family laugh even in tough times.

   I play with my family every chance I get.

Career/Sport Goals:

Outcome Goals:

1. I have built up a company that continues to thrive even though I've semi-retired.

   #### Process Goals:

   I work 20 hours per week.

I did and do everything I could and can to be the best CEO. I make decisions that are in the best interest of the company.

Friendship Goals:

Outcome Goals:

1. I have lots of friends that like to have fun.

   ### Process Goals:

   I'm fun to be around and I'm always myself with my friends.

2. I have close friends who I can turn to when I need them.

   ### Process Goals:

   I'm loyal to my good friends.

Physical/Mental Health Goals:

Outcome Goals:

1. I've gotten through my career and maintained my health.

   ### Process Goals:

   I listen to my body and give it what it needs.

2. I'm healthy and strong.

   ### Process Goals:

   I exercise for at least 30 minutes every day.

   I eat food that is good for me every day for at least 2 of 3 meals.

Personal Development/Growth/Spiritual Goals:

Outcome Goals:

1. I'm the best I can be with whatever I'm focusing on.

   ### Process Goals:

   I read at least 30 minutes per day.

   I keep an open mind and learn as much as I can every day.

2. I'm connected with a higher power.

    Process Goals:

    I pray daily and attend church weekly.

Financial Goals:

Outcome Goals:

1. I'm financially independent.

    Process Goals:

    I live below my means.

    I invest my money wisely by taking the advice from trusted sources.

2. I've provided for my kids so they can feel free to pursue their dreams.

    Process Goals:

    I live below my means.

    I invest my money wisely by taking the advice from trusted sources.

Now it's time for you to write down your Long-Term/Retirement Goals. Fill in the form below or download printable goal sheets at FriesenPerformance.com/Achieve-Bonus-Materials.

Family Goals

Outcome Goals:

1._____

    Process Goals:

    _____

    _____

2._____

    Process Goals:

    _____

    _____

3._____

    Process Goals:

    _____

    _____

4._____

    Process Goals:

    _____

    _____

Career/Sport Goals

Outcome Goals:

1._____

    Process Goals:

    _____

    _____

2._____

    Process Goals:

    _____

3._____

    Process Goals:

_____

_____

4. _____

    Process Goals:

_____

_____

Friendship Goals

Outcome Goals:

1._____

    Process Goals:

_____

_____

2. _____

    Process Goals:

_____

_____

3._____

    Process Goals:

_____

_____

4. _____

    Process Goals:

_____

_____

Physical/Mental Health Goals

Outcome Goals:

1._____

    Process Goals:

    _____

    _____

2._____

    Process Goals:

    _____

    _____

3._____

    Process Goals:

    _____

    _____

4._____

    Process Goals:

    _____

    _____

Personal Development/Growth/Spiritual Goals

Outcome Goals:

1._____

    Process Goals:

    _____

    _____

2._____

    Process Goals:

    _____

3._____

    Process Goals:

4._____

    Process Goals:

Financial Goals

Outcome Goals:

1._____

    Process Goals:

2._____

    Process Goals:

3._____

    Process Goals:

4._____

    Process Goals:

Other Goals

Outcome Goals:

1._____

    Process Goals:

_____

_____

2. _____

    Process Goals:

_____

_____

3._____

    Process Goals:

_____

_____

4. _____

    Process Goals:

_____

_____

ESTABLISHING MILEPOSTS

Now you are to look at your long-term goals and ask yourself what you need to do in the medium-term all the way to-daily term to reach your long-term goals. You may also have other goals that are still in line with your values and mission, but are not reflected in your long-term goals. Feel free to add them.

You can download the worksheets for this section at FriesenPerformance.com/Achieve-Bonus-Materials.

Please do the same as above for each section. Try to write in the first person and use the present tense when possible. You will notice they become more and more SMART as you get down to your monthly, weekly, and daily goals. But you may still have goals that are expressions of how you want to be, or your values, which are harder to quantify.

Do your best to make them specific, measurable, achievable, relevant, and time-bound. For example, you may have an outcome goal to have a positive relationship with your family. When it comes to setting your monthly process goals, you may set the following process goals:

- I call my parents once per week.

- When my partner tells me about his/her problems, I stop what I'm doing and focus my attention on them for as long as they need.

- When I pick my son up from school, I play with him for at least 1 hour with my phone off.

Now it's your turn. Try to stick to the guidelines set out above and write in your outcome and process goals for each time period below on the online worksheets FriesenPerformance.com/Achieve-Bonus-Materials:

- MEDIUM TERM OR 10-YEAR GOALS

- 5-YEAR GOALS

- 1-YEAR GOALS

- 6-MONTH GOALS

- 1-MONTH GOALS

- 1-WEEK GOALS

- DAILY GOALS

Don't just file these away! Whenever a new opportunity arises, a request comes in from others, or anything else crops up that may take your time and energy, ask yourself if it fits into your values, goals, and mission. If so, then all is good. If not, ask yourself if your current goals need updating, or if this new activity is taking time and energy away from what it truly important to you.

HOW TO STAY FOCUSED ON YOUR GOALS

IMAGINE REACHING YOUR GOAL

This is where a lot of self-help books get things wrong. Many of these books urge you to visualize yourself achieving your goals with all their associated glory. I see this a lot with coaches, athletes, and entrepreneurs.

Many athletes tell me they've used visualization before. When I ask what they visualize, they almost invariably tell me they see themselves winning and maybe imagine how great it will feel. This strategy is only partially wrong. Sure, it probably makes you feel good and boosts your confidence for a few moments. It's a great first step. But this is not enough. To fully take advantage of the power of imagery you need to be a little more realistic and strategic.

One of the first things to understand is that when you imagine yourself in a scenario vividly enough, your brain has a hard time distinguishing reality from fantasy. In fact, amazing MRI research has found that just by repeatedly imagining carrying out an action there is measurable increases in thickness in the part of the brain responsible for that action.[41]

The trick is to make it as real as possible by using most of your senses. There is a reason why psychologists don't refer to it as "visualization" anymore. It is referred to as imagery, as this has a broader meaning in terms of your senses. You should not only imagine what you see with your eyes, but also what you will hear, feel emotionally, sense with your body, and even what you may smell or taste! The more senses you engage, the more your brain thinks it really happened.

---

[41] Pascual-Leone (1996). Reorganization of cortical motor outputs in the acquisition of new motor skills. In Recent Advances in Clinical Neurophysiology, Editors: Kinura & Shibasaki, pp. 304–3088.

Imagining yourself effortlessly launching your product or winning in your sport doesn't really help you achieve the goal. Instead, you need to vividly imagine facing the many probable and even improbable challenges, obstacles, and pain you could possibly face. The trick is to vividly imagine yourself successfully navigating these.

If you simply imagine yourself easily achieving your goal, you may become overconfident. This overconfidence can lull you into under-preparation and lead you to underestimate your competition or how hard something is going to be. This can make you complacent. Your motivation drops. Then, when you show up at the event, you get blindsided when you suddenly realize you underestimated your competition or what you had to do, and thus you're under-prepared.

Remember, self-doubt can be your friend. Why? Because it motivates you to avoid danger and improve.

So there is a difference between imagining the end result of achieving your goal or that it will be easy, and imagining and believing that you will achieve your goal, despite any obstacles that get in your way. The former hinders you and the latter helps you achieve the goal.

So when I was defending my Ph.D., I didn't imagine myself walking in there, charming the committee, feeling pure confidence, answering all the questions with ease, and them stopping the defense early to congratulate me on obtaining my degree. No. I imagined going through a war. I imagined tough questions, my PowerPoint slides not working, being nervous as hell, being cross-examined for five hours straight and *despite this*, successfully dealing with it and coming out on top in the end.

If I convinced myself that my Ph.D. defense was going to be a breeze, I would have become overconfident and then under-prepared. I would then have been blindsided by what actually happened during the defense. The reality was that I was nervous as heck and there was one committee member who seemed to be doing their best to trip me up and set me up for failure.

Imagining worst-case scenarios and coming up with plans for how you might overcome them is the key. This is where using "if X, then Y" solutions can be helpful. This will be described in more detail in the next chapter. But briefly, it involves setting goals and preparing for different challenges by coming up with a plan of action, "If X happens, then I will do Y."

So before my defense, I told myself "if I feel really anxious during the defense, then I'll remind myself that this is totally normal, reflects my passion, and that it can improve my performance." I also prepared by telling myself that "if committee members are giving me a hard time or asking challenging questions, then I'll remind myself that I know more about my dissertation than they do, and that the harder my defense is, the bigger the sense of accomplishment I'll feel once I pass."

So you vividly imagine yourself implementing your plans successfully and how great it will feel when you come out on top. It's at this point where you should bask in the glory and imagine all the great things that can happen when you achieve your goal. To maximize your success, you should use this imagery strategy for both your longer-term and shorter-term outcome and process goals.

WRITE IT DOWN; VISIT IT OFTEN

You're going to run into obstacles when trying to achieve your goals. These may be external, like unsupportive friends or family, or internal like self-doubts and self-sabotage from fear of failure. And the higher your standing on the Basic Personality Tendency of Negative Emotions, the more you will be prone to the latter.

Without specific goals that are recorded in some way, your chances of getting the outcomes you desire are much lower. You should write out your goals and have them in a place that is visible or easily accessible like on your phone as a daily alarm, on your fridge, on your wall or computer monitor, as wallpaper on your computer, on your bathroom mirror, or on your car's dashboard.

You may also want to look into having a physical journal where you record your goals and progress. One great example of this comes from entrepreneur guru, John Lee Dumas' product, The Freedom Journal (http://thefreedomjournal.com/). This is more than a journal, as it guides you through many of the things described in this chapter, including how to establish SMART goals, setting short- and long-term goals, reviewing your goals at regular intervals, and keeping yourself accountable.

Having clear goals that are written down will do a number of things. For one, it will force you to track how much progress you've made toward a goal. It also motivates you to take consistent action. It will keep you focused on what you need to be doing, and prevent you from getting sidetracked by something else.

Have you ever had the experience where something becomes important to you and then suddenly you start seeing instances of it everywhere? Maybe a friend bought a nice blue Jeep that you thought was awesome. You think they are pretty rare, until you start to see Jeeps everywhere over the next few days, with a number of them being blue.

Our brains are constantly deciding what information to focus on and what information to ignore. This applies to internal information like our thoughts, and to external information like what we notice in our environment. Having your goals written out where you can review them regularly will help keep your brain primed to pay attention to the things that will bring you closer to your goals, and ignore things that will not help you reach your goals.

SHARE YOUR GOALS WITH OTHERS

Goals are contagious and making public statements about your goals can be motivating. For example, I wanted to write this book for a number of years, but it really wasn't until I put my money where my mouth was and finally made a public declaration and commitment that I would write this book, that I made it happen.

A great example of this is Ted Ryce's Legendary Life Movement. Ryce developed a simple process that involves writing your goal on a card and then making a public declaration. The process is simple:

1. Write your goal down on the "What I'll do to live a legendary life" card.

2. Take a picture of yourself holding the card with your goal clearly written out.

3. Post your picture on your social media accounts and on Facebook.com/LegendaryLifePod

4. Carry the card with you until you reach your goal, or put it in a place where you will see it daily (e.g., on your wall, as your smartphone's wallpaper, on your bathroom mirror, or on your steering wheel).

5. Once you've achieved your goal, post a picture on your social media accounts with you holding your original card with a giant check-mark over it.

You can get these cards here: https://goo.gl/YDFuuP

KEEP SCORE AND COLLECT TROPHIES

Without noting and celebrating your progress, including daily advances, you'll easily be discouraged. You need to take it one day, one week, one month, and one year at a time. You need to focus on what you want in the end and then work your way backwards. Otherwise, you'll simply look at the end goal and where you are at today and feel discouraged.

When I was completing my Ph.D. dissertation, I met and heard about many fellow graduate students who had been working on their dissertations for a decade or more! A decade!! The idea that I might still be in school for another decade scared the tar out of me. I told myself there was no way I was going to take more than seven years to do both my clinical psychology master's degree and Ph.D. Seven years was generally the minimum time needed to complete all the requirements.

181

So when I first started graduate school and had to pick a username for my email address, I purposely chose the number 7 to serve as a constant reminder of the maximum number of years I was going to spend to complete the program.

Knowing how easily I could forget how much progress I had made, I also made a point to rename my master's thesis and dissertation documents with the date each time I worked on them. So in the drafts folder on my computer, I had over one hundred versions that were constant reminders of how far I had come.

So you need to know where you're going, and then take note of your progress along the way. This prevents discouragement and overwhelm, and helps you feel a sense of progress and accomplishment. It also helps you figure out where you're going wrong. There is a famous quote that appears to be falsely attributed to Albert Einstein that is relevant here: "The definition of insanity is doing the same thing over and over again, but expecting different results." Tracking progress will help you determine whether you are on the right track or not.

There are many ways to track progress. You can have a document where you list all your completed goals. This can be done on your calendar with big checkmarks or highlights denoting the goals that have been completed. You may even have a coach or accountability buddy who helps you review everything you've accomplished and guard against the tendency to focus only on what you haven't accomplished.

Ideally, try to track your progress at regular intervals — daily, weekly, monthly, quarterly, or yearly — depending on the goal. But make sure you also think about what needs to be done next. In fact, Heidi Halvorson summarizes research showing that focusing too much on how much you've progressed, while not also focusing on what remains to be done, actually reduces your motivation to keep working toward the goal.[42] It can lead to too much of a sense of accomplishment and cause you to take your foot off the gas. So definitely acknowledge your progress, but *don't forget* to review what you still

---

[42] Halvorson (2010). Succeed: How We Can Reach Our Goals.

have to do to accomplish the goal.

Keep in mind, you're never going to be able to perfectly articulate how you are going to reach your long-term goals. You'll never see the full path and that's ok. Your path will be unpredictably indirect and bumpy. You must take one day at a time. Although persistence is key to achieving goals, you have to regularly and realistically appraise your goals to make sure they are leading you down the right path. You need to ask yourself, "Is what I'm doing bringing me closer to my long-term goals? My mission? My purpose?"

If your answer is 'no,' then either tweak what you're doing, change your strategy, or change your goal. Sometimes you have to know when to quit. Sometimes, continuing to pursue a goal ends up being incompatible with a bigger goal you have. I'll give you a personal example.

At one point recently, I had to make a hard decision about whether to keep playing hockey as a goalie. Playing competitively was important to me for several reasons. It was fun and another way of staying fit that didn't seem like exercise. It also helped keep fresh in my mind what it's like to battle the ups and downs that come with performing in sport and use the skills I was teaching high achieving athletes I worked with.

I loved playing, but over the years I developed back pain that worsened and worsened. An MRI of my back revealed a number of herniated discs, some worse than others. Technically, I could keep playing through the pain and it may or may not get much worse. It's a gamble.

But I had to think long and hard about how doing so might conflict with a longer-term goal I have of living a long, healthy, and happy life. In my work as a psychologist, I've assessed and treated hundreds of people with chronic pain, mostly lower back pain. I've seen how such pain can destroy a patient's quality of life. I had many reasons why I wanted to keep playing hockey, but I had to focus on my long-term goals, and drop the short-term goal of playing hockey. Life is all about choices.

KNOWING WHEN TO REASSESS GOALS AND PLANS

I'm a firm believer in seriously taking time to review your mission, purpose, and goals at the turn of the year. This is an absolute must. Ideally, you should take a vacation from your daily grind to do this. The next step is to review all of your goals once a month. It's usually easiest to do this at the end of the month.

Of course, you're not just reviewing your goals. You want to check in with yourself to make sure these goals are still the right goals for you, or the right goals to be focusing on at this point in time.

You'll find that some of your goals for the month were accomplished and you should find a way to mark these accomplishments. One way is to take your written-out goals and move them to another file or folder labeled Completed Goals or Achievements, or whatever you like. You should review these about every six months to help you see how far you've come.

In your review, you may end up slightly altering or changing goals altogether. Remember, goals are fluid and you need to be flexible. If your goal was to beat your best time in your track event within the month, but you tore your ACL, this goal needs to be abandoned and moved into the 1-Year Goals list.

Next, plan your outcome and process goals for the coming month and plan out when and how you will achieve them.

Then, each week pick a day to review your past week and the week to come. Take 10 to 30 minutes to do this. Look at your goals from the week before and evaluate how well you did. Then, look ahead at the week to come and schedule where and when you will work on your goals.

This is undoubtedly superior to scheduling on a daily basis, a process that will inevitably get you caught up in what Stephen Covey refers to as "The thick of thin things." Covey notes that "things which matter most must never be at the mercy of things which matter least." With daily planning, you will get caught up in things that are not in line with your overall mission, purpose, values, and goals.

When you plan out the week, you need to schedule non-negotiable times when you're going to work on things that will bring you closer to your goals. These are activities that are important, but often not urgent. Still, they require us to take action to make them happen. If we don't act, we will end up living our lives at the whims of others. We'll become slaves to things that may not be in our best interests.

For example, some athletes say they want to make it big and play lip service to the idea that the mental game is important. But they never seem to get around to doing what is needed to improve their mental game. Life just gets in the way. They have practice, training sessions, possibly school or jobs, a social life, and more. These are all important, but we need to realize we are making a choice. And that's okay as long as we are aware we are making that choice.

As I said at the beginning of this book, you want to be able to look yourself in the mirror and say you did everything you could to achieve your dream. We all fall victim to getting caught up in things that seem important, but really aren't. That's why we need to repeatedly keep in touch with our overall mission, values, and goals. And we need to plan what we are going to do on a yearly, monthly, weekly, and even daily basis.

CONCLUSION

You now have everything in place. You now have some goals that are in line with your personality, values, strengths, interests, and most importantly, your purpose or mission.

In the next chapter, you'll learn how to put your goals into action and deal with any stumbling blocks on a day-to-day basis. I will help you understand what it takes to stay motivated, productive, and effective.

Resources

Succeed: How We Can Reach Our Goals by Heidi Halvorson, Ph.D.:
http://goo.gl/qwdLq4

First Things First by Covey, Merrill, & Merill: http://goo.gl/pcUHwq

The Freedom Journal, John Lee Dumas: http://thefreedomjournal.com

The Legendary Life Movement, Ted Ryce:
   http://FriesenPerformance.com.legendarylifepodcast.com

BONUS MATERIAL

Visit FriesenPerformance.com/Achieve-Bonus-Materials to download your Goals Worksheets.

STEP 6

MAKING IT HAPPEN!

Chapter 14

HOW TO WALK
THE PATH TO SUCCESS

A dream doesn't become reality through magic; it takes sweat,
determination and hard work.

— Colin Powell

Ideas are easy. Implementation is hard.

— Guy Kawasaki

At this point, you should know a lot more about yourself and what you are
trying to achieve. You've figured out your Basic Personality Tendencies,
values, strengths, interests, purpose, mission, and goals.

Now comes the hard part: putting in the hard work to make your goals
a reality. This is where many of us crumble. You may know what you want,
but have no idea how to make it happen on a daily basis. This chapter will
help you make it happen even if you are not high on Motivation.

Some of the strategies to follow may be applicable to you and some may
not. The metric for your success is when you do your weekly, monthly,
semi-annual, and annual reviews of your progress. At each of these intervals,
you're going to ask yourself how you're coming along in terms of your goals
and mission.

Is the To-Do List Dead?

As noted in the last chapter, at regular intervals you need to review and plan your goals and how you are going to achieve them. We stopped at weekly planning. The problem with stopping at weekly planning is that we often get caught up in all sorts of things that may or may not be in line with our values, goals, and mission. How do we prevent this from happening? Use a to-do list.

Although some productivity books say that to-do lists are a thing of the past, I disagree. Of course, I think we can all agree that making to-do lists that are not informed by your values, mission, and long-range goals won't help you achieve the right goals. But to-do lists have a number of useful functions.

Simply having your tasks written out, with old fashion pen or pencil or electronically, serves to free up your brain's RAM, known as working memory. Your working memory is your brain's ability to keep information front-and-center so that you can work on it for short periods of time.

Some cognitive neuroscientists have argued that working memory is *the* key to intelligence. They believe it is the core cognitive ability that underlies almost all of our cognitive powers. There is some evidence that you can improve your working memory with training, but it's generally limited in capacity.

Working memory, along with your brain's ability to process information quickly, are part of a more global cognitive ability known as cognitive efficiency. Poor cognitive efficiency acts as a bottleneck for your other cognitive abilities like memory, language, and problem-solving. So you don't want to clog up your working memory with tasks you are trying to remember to do. Writing things down on a to-do list frees up your brain's working memory capacity, which allows you to use it for tasks you want to be focused on.

In addition to weekly tracking of progress toward goals, you need to track small accomplishments. Again, this is where the to-do list comes in.

The act of physically checking off boxes and crossing things out serves an important psychological function. You're telling your brain that you're "done" with that task. This allows your brain to take any information about the task out of working memory, freeing it up for more pressing tasks.

It also gives you a feeling of accomplishment, of moving forward, and activates your brain's dopamine reward system. So, in other words, it helps keep motivation and morale strong and also just feels good.

It's also best to finish tasks or to get some form of "closure" on something you're working on before moving on to the next task or finishing your day. Otherwise, it may tend to linger in your working memory and affect your performance later. This is known as Attentional Residue.[43]

If you leave a bunch of unfinished tasks, you feel a diminished sense of competence and accomplishment, even though you recognize that you worked hard all day. Your brain needs this reward to keep going. Otherwise you'll end up procrastinating or feeling overwhelmed. This will wreak havoc on your motivation. This is why you have to break down your big goals into smaller and smaller tasks.

Each night look over your weekly plan for what you scheduled for the next day, and then make a to-do list. When you do this the night before, there is still distance and perspective on the next day.

If you only check your plan or make your to-do list in the morning, you may already have been bombarded with emails and other things that make it difficult to stick to your weekly plan. You may also feel tired or unmotivated when you wake up in the morning. It helps to have a set of written reminders of what you said you would tackle that day. And when you wake up, you've already completed the most important task for the day, making your to-do list!

---

[43] Leroy (2009). Why is it so hard to do my work? The challenge of attention residue when switching between work tasks. Organizational Behavior and Human Decision Processes, 109(2), 168-181.

This doesn't mean looking at your long-term goals here. You're welcome to, of course, but if you are reviewing these on a weekly basis, it isn't necessary. You're looking at your goals for the week and day.

Each morning, begin with a look at your written-out to-do list that was developed with your weekly plan in mind when you had more perspective the evening before. Do this before you check your email or voicemail or get caught up in any time-consuming tasks. If you wait to check your to-do list after doing these activities, you may get sucked down a rabbit hole of seemingly urgent, but possibly unimportant, tasks when it comes to your goals and mission. Learn to say 'no' to these things and say 'yes' to your bigger goals. The more you do this, the easier it will become.

At the same time, important things that are urgent will crop up. These are things you have to deal with promptly to prevent them from leading to even bigger problems. If you have an urgent deadline at work, it could be career suicide to put it off so you can focus on your bigger goals. Or maybe you're an athlete and you notice a strange pain in your knee while training. Even though your goal may be to train at a certain intensity a set number of times each week, it would be foolish to push through the pain. It may even be career-ending. Or you get a call that a loved one is in the hospital. I think we can all agree that your to-do list can wait. So you have to be somewhat flexible.

At regular intervals throughout the day, check your to-do list and see how you're doing. One way to do this is to program a repeating reminder into your smartphone. It can be as simple as having it go off at 9 a.m., 1 p.m., and 3 p.m., or at whatever intervals work within your schedule, with the message "**to do list!**" That should be enough to remind you to check your list.

WHERE THERE'S A WILL, THERE'S A WAY

You may have heard something about willpower. Willpower refers to your ability to delay gratification and resist short-term temptations in order to meet your longer-term goals. It's been getting a lot of press these days, largely because of the work of psychologists Roy Baumeister, Kelly McGonigal, and their colleagues.

You may have noticed that the definition of willpower is pretty similar to the Basic Personality Tendency of Motivation. You also may have heard of popular related terms like "grit" and "self-control." The University of Pennsylvania's positive psychologist Angela Duckworth defines grit as the tendency to sustain interest in and effort toward very long-term goals, and self-control as the ability to modulate impulses in the presence of momentarily gratifying temptations or diversions. It turns out, willpower, grit, and self-control are all sub-traits of the larger Basic Personality Tendency of Motivation.[44]

There are a number of keys to high achievement, including having willpower and self-control. Higher levels of willpower in children predict numerous positive outcomes even into adulthood. Stronger willpower is related to higher or better grades, rates of sobriety, income, physical health, mental health, and self-esteem.[45,46]

Like most Basic Personality Tendencies, there is room to improve your willpower through a combination of knowing how it works, working around it, and strengthening it.

You should keep in mind that we all have difficulties getting ourselves to do things we don't feel like doing, or stopping ourselves from doing things we know we shouldn't be doing. Those of you who are average to low in the Basic Personality Tendency of Motivation will find this even harder. So you should devote even more attention to this section. This is especially true with getting yourself to do things you know you should be doing, as

---

[44] See Angela Duckworth's statement on the relationship between grit, self-control and the Basic Personality Tendency of Motivation/Self-Control (referred to as Conscientiousness) here: https://goo.gl/Gq7120

[45] Moffitt et al. (2011). A gradient of childhood self-control predicts health, wealth, and public safety. Proceedings of the National Academy of Sciences, 108, 2693-2698.

[46] See APA's What You Need To Know about Willpower: The Science of Self-Control: http://goo.gl/yluyQ5

this is a motivational issue and is more closely tied to the concept of willpower. For example, getting yourself to wake up early to work out will be harder for you.

WILLPOWER & NEGATIVE EMOTIONS

Another key to high achievement relates to your ability to handle negative emotions and stress, which will be the focus of one of the upcoming books in this series. If you are average to high on Negative Emotions, learning to handle stress should be a major focus of your personal development if you want to be happy and achieve big goals.

Although willpower is mostly related to the Basic Personality Tendency of Motivation, it's also related to Negative Emotions, though to a lesser extent. Specifically, many personality psychologists argue that stopping yourself from doing something you know you shouldn't do is more of an emotional issue than a motivational challenge. I'm referring to having trouble stopping yourself from doing things like overeating, eating unhealthy foods, overspending, over-drinking, smoking, or gambling. It's mainly emotional because you may engage in these behaviors to improve your mood, or you struggle to tolerate the negative emotions that accompany not giving in to your urges.

This means that learning to better tolerate negative emotions and stress will increase your willpower. So if you are average to high on Negative Emotions, you too should pay special attention to the strategies in this section.

Recall that willpower refers to your ability to delay gratification and resist short-term temptations in order to meet your longer-term goals. This requires a more logical or rational way of thinking. It requires us to not get swept away by emotions.

When we do get caught-up in high levels of negative emotions, the Amygdala Hijack kicks in. Recall that the amygdala is deep within your brain and is part of the emotional system, known as the limbic system. Your prefrontal cortex is the home of your more logical thinking system. When negative emotions or urges arise, our limbic system may get too amped and "hijack" the prefrontal cortex, essentially preventing us from thinking rationally.

I once worked with a professional hockey player who was extremely talented but repeatedly underperformed whenever something didn't go his way on the ice. When he would get checked or tripped by another player, he would "see red" and could no longer think rationally about what he needed to be doing. His logical, prefrontal cortex was essentially "shut down" by his limbic system and he would take bad penalties or just be out of the flow of the game. Attempts by coaches and teammates to calm him down only made him angrier, as in those moments he felt they "didn't understand." After the games, though, he was easily able to see how "ridiculous" his behaviors were.

So willpower can be viewed as the ability to regulate your thoughts, feelings, and behaviors. The good news is you can learn to work around and even improve your willpower.

WILLPOWER IS A LIMITED RESOURCE

One of the first things you need to understand is that your willpower is a limited resource. You can imagine it as a gas tank that usually starts off the day being relatively full. It then gradually goes down over the course of the day.[47]

You're using this limited resource a lot more than you think. Even making simple decisions like what to wear in the morning depletes your willpower. This is why some researchers refer to this as "decision fatigue." Whenever you're at the coffee shop and find yourself looking at the donut and the 450-calorie mocha latte with cream and sugar, but instead go for the green tea and protein bar, your willpower is being sapped. Even closing your

---

[47] Baumeister et al. (1998). Ego depletion: is the active self a limited resource? Journal of Personality and Social Psychology, 74, 1252-1265.

email window or social media feed to get down to work depletes your willpower.

Research has shown that the more we use our willpower, the more energy is used by our brains. This energy is in the form of our brain's primary fuel, glucose. The brain is a glucose hog. Despite making up only 2 percent of the body's weight, it consumes 20 percent of its energy.

When we exert self-control, our brains gobble up even more glucose, possibly more than it can replenish. Research has found that when our willpower has been repeatedly challenged, it becomes depleted. This correlates with lower blood glucose levels and reduced activity in the rational part of the brain, the prefrontal cortex. The good news is that consumption of foods high in glucose can give our willpower a short boost.[48] Even better, of course, is to eat the foods that keep our bodies fixed with a nice, steady supply of fuel. More on this in the upcoming books in this series.

How to Limit the Willpower Drain

Motivation is what gets you started. Habit is what keeps you going.
— Jim Ryun

A problem that trips up many people with lots of motivation is trying to tackle too many big goals or make too many big changes at once. This is especially problematic for those who are high on the Basic Personality Tendency of Motivation.

Understand that working on your goals or making changes in your life takes a lot of willpower and self-control. So if you find yourself struggling to keep up with your daily goals, check to see if you aren't trying to do too many things at once. If so, try to cut back your less urgent goals for a limited time — let's say a month or two — and see how that goes. It should free up more willpower.

---

[48] Gailliot et al. (2007). Self-control relies on glucose as a limited energy source: willpower is more than a metaphor. Journal of Personality and Social Psychology, 92, 325-336.

After you've engaged in a new behavior for a longer period of time, like getting up 30 minutes earlier each morning, the control of the behavior moves from the effortful and conscious outer part of your brain to the more automatic and unconscious deeper parts of your brain. When this happens, the new behavior no longer requires as much willpower. It becomes an automatic habit.

Think of something as simple as learning to skate or dribble a basketball. When you were first learning to do these things, it took a lot of conscious mental energy. It also took a lot of willpower and self-control to not go back to easier moves like just gliding around a turn instead of doing crossovers while skating or traveling in basketball by taking a few steps without dribbling the ball.

When you were learning these skills, you had to engage your willpower and self-control not to go back to bad habits. But once you practiced enough, these behaviors no longer took much conscious effort or willpower, as they were relegated to the deeper, more automatic procedural parts of your brain. Once you've engaged in a behavior long enough, it no longer requires willpower. It is now a habit.

SOME SIMPLE WILLPOWER 'HACKS'

Limit your use of willpower: The best strategy to maintain your willpower is simply to reduce the number of times you have to exert self-control or make decisions. When I work with elite athletes competing in major events, we make sure they get to their events a few days early, not only to acclimatize to the environment, but also to set things up so they don't have to exert much willpower, self-control, or make many decisions close to competition.

We make sure almost everything is pre-decided at least for the day before and the day of competition. This includes even simple things such as when they're going to wake up, what they're going to wear, what they're going to eat, what time they're going to leave for the competition, or exactly how they are going to get to the venue. These are all pre-set so they can conserve their mental energy by not having to draw on the limited resource of willpower.

This strategy holds true for your everyday decisions as well. If your plan is to get up at 6 a.m. tomorrow to work out, get everything ready the night before. Get out your gym clothes, equipment, supplements, and such so you don't have to waste time and energy looking for these things or trying to make any decisions the next morning.

The same goes for more cognitive tasks like writing a report or book. If tomorrow you plan to work on your project for three hours, clear your desk the day before, decide what you're going to do if the phone rings or you get an "urgent" email about something that may or may not be urgent. You need to imagine yourself dealing with these effectively. Taking this step is essential to sticking to your plan and achieving your goals.

For some athletes I work with who have to make weight for competition, like wrestling and mixed martial arts, one of the hardest things they have to do is exert willpower and self-control to stick to a strict diet. The body likes to fight back when we try to stick to a dietary regimen.

The body is generally pre-programmed to stay at a particular weight and does everything in its power to prevent rapid changes, especially weight loss, as it is more dangerous to survival in the short term than weight gain. Whenever we try to cut back on calories, the brain sets off a number of processes to prevent weight loss, which includes making you obsess about food. It takes an unbelievable amount of willpower to stay on a strict diet, which is one reason diets don't work in the long term. As the day goes on, denying yourself the calories your body craves uses up a lot of the willpower gas tank.

Most of us can relate to this, especially if we are average-to-high on Negative Emotions, or average-to-low on Motivation. Think of how easy it is not to eat that ice cream in your fridge for breakfast even though you're starving. But resisting the urge to eat that same ice cream when you're not even hungry at 10 p.m. is next to impossible for many people. The trick here is to engineer your environment to prevent this from happening.

One strategy is to make it much harder to get your hands on the offending food. So at the very least, bury it deep in your freezer! Better yet, put it in the freezer in your basement. Even better than that, of course, is simply to not have it in the house. So you want to make it a pain in the ass to get a hold of.

As disciplined as I am, even I had this exact problem. Almost every night I craved ice cream and was almost powerless to stop myself from eating it. Because of my history of being on the higher side of Negative Emotions temperamentally, it should come as no surprise that this would be a potential weakness for me.

Don't get me wrong, eating ice cream a few nights a week isn't going to kill you. But I wanted it *every* night. So I did two things. Given we don't own a second freezer in the basement or garage, putting it there was not an option. Instead, I purchased only one smaller tub of Ben & Jerry's or Haagen Das per week. When this was split with my wife, there was no way it would last more than two nights.

You may be asking, "What did you do on the other nights?" Well, what I did was drink a cup of decaf tea or coffee and have one of my favorite protein bars. Once I consumed these, I usually had no more cravings. And if I did have cravings, I worked on tolerating the discomfort, which is something I will have more to say about in the upcoming books in this series.

Use If-Then Statements: Another strategy is to use the "if-then" statements I will discuss below with goal implementation. Basically, you just plan for what you are going to do when a specific situation arises. If you're dieting and trying to make weight and your partner or buddy shows up with some Haagen Das, you've already prepared in your mind what you're going to do. So it would look like this:

Before being confronted with a situation like this, you write down or at least say to yourself "*if* I get confronted with a food that is not part of my diet plan, like ice-cream, I will drink a decaf coffee and have a protein bar." Researchers have found this technique to be very effective in improving self-control, even when your willpower is depleted! Having the plan in mind ahead of time requires much less willpower to make the more appropriate choice.

Build-up Willpower: Think of willpower as a muscle. The more we work it, the more fatigued it gets. The flip side is that the more you exercise willpower, the stronger it gets.[49] There are different ways of doing this. Resisting little temptations each day, like pushing your plate away before you are totally full, can strengthen your willpower.

You can also get yourself to do things that are hard or that you're not dying to do each day. One strategy that I and some of my clients use is to take a cold shower each morning. Doing things that are uncomfortable or difficult, like taking a cold shower, is bloody hard to do! Before we do something hard, our brains often tell us that we won't be able to handle it or it will be too hard. Usually, we listen to this little voice and obey it.

Despite doing this for almost a year, my mind still tries to convince me that I can't do it each morning. But this argument is now weak. What I do is thank my mind for doing what it is designed to do, which is to help me avoid pain — then do it anyway. This builds self-confidence and self-efficacy in addition to willpower and serves to reduce the power my negative predictions have over me. By doing hard things every day, you will increase your willpower and repeatedly show yourself that you are more than your momentary thoughts and feelings.

Exercising your willpower doesn't just increase your willpower for the task you exerted control over. There is a spillover effect and your ability to exert self-control in other situations improves.[50] So successfully sticking to your goals and plans breeds more success.

---

[49] Oaten & Cheng (2006). Longitudinal gains in self-regulation from physical exercise. British Journal of Health Psychology, 11, 717-733.

[50] Muraven et al. (1999). Longitudinal improvement of self-regulation through practice: building self-control strength through repeated exercise. Journal of Social Psychology, 139, 446-45

Boosting Willpower When It's Depleted: Researchers have found that willpower is never really totally exhausted. But it gets harder and harder to utilize as it becomes depleted.

The good news is you can get a boost by drawing on your motivation or the reasons why you need to use your willpower.[51] And there is significantly less willpower depletion when you use it for reasons that are in line with your values, passions, goals, and purpose!

When you feel the need to exert willpower for reasons that are contrary to your mission, values, and goals, such as when you try to please others or for some other external reason, your willpower becomes depleted faster. So use the strategies in this book to make sure you're working toward the right goals. This will help ensure that your willpower remains as strong as possible.

We also know that the willpower depletion effect is minimized when you're in a good mood when exerting self-control. So it's easier to exert your willpower when you feel good or have positive and supportive family and friends around you who make you feel good.[52]

Similarly, how you view a situation, or your beliefs and attitudes, can mitigate willpower depletion. For example, if you find it hard to get yourself to work out due to willpower depletion, you can remind yourself how you will feel good about getting closer to your goals if you do exercise. When you do this, the act will have less of a depleting effect on your willpower.

Other things that lift your mood like listening to your favorite music can also temporarily boost your willpower. So feel free to blast your favorite tunes when you feel the need for a willpower boost.[53]

---

[51] Muraven & Slessareva (2003). Mechanism of self-control failure: Motivation and limited resources. Personality and Social Psychology Bulletin, 29, 894–906.
[52] Tice et al. (2007). Restoring the self: Positive affect helps improve self-regulation following ego depletion. Journal of Experimental Social Psychology 43(3), 379-384.
[53] See the work of Kathleen Martin Ginis, Ph.D.: http://goo.gl/FJEH7p
and Costas Karageorghis, Ph.D.: http://goo.gl/AwQQOx

Also, as noted earlier, consumption of foods high in glucose can give our willpower a short boost. Even better of course is to eat the right foods that give your body a nice steady supply of glucose. But in times of need, sucking on a sugary candy might do the trick.

Another strategy to increase your willpower when it's already depleted is to just think of someone who has a lot of willpower.[54] Maybe you're a combat athlete training and find yourself wanting to give up due to exhaustion. Thinking of your upcoming opponent continuing to train despite their fatigue can motivate you. Or you can imagine someone you admire and how they wouldn't give up or give in to temptations in the situation you are in.

How to Make 'If-Then' Plans

Another great strategy to keep you on track toward your goals is to have "if-then" plans. This strategy has been brought up a number of times in this book for good reason. It works. It has been well researched and is highlighted in Heidi Grant Halvorson's book titled *Succeed*.

This involves having specific plans for when you are going to work towards your goals, and can help you prepare for things that can get in the way. It basically refers to the idea that you plan ahead by thinking: "If X happens, then I will do Y." So, for example, when you plan your week, think of the various actions you want to take or any obstacles that may come up. Then rephrase it with "if-then." Here are some examples:

- "If it's Tuesday, Thursday, or Sunday, I will wake up at 6:30 a.m. and do cardio."

- "If my phone rings during my dedicated time for working on my big goals, I'll let it go to voicemail."

---

[54] vanDellen & Hoyle (2010). Regulatory accessibility and social influences on state self-control. Peronality and Social Psychology Bulletin, 36(2), 251-263.

- "If I'm driving in the car alone, I will do my breathing exercises for at least five minutes" (more on this on my website and in the upcoming books in this series).

Remember, our brains like to be told what to do, not what *not* to do. If you use "if-then" plans, your brain will know when to do something, where to do it, and/or what to do if a specific situation arises. Less willpower will be used because the "decision" has already been made. According to Halvorson, there are hundreds of studies that have been done on "if-then" planning.[55] The results? On average, there are increased rates of goal attainment and productivity of 200 to 300 percent! So using this strategy will make sticking to your plans and goals easier for you.

WHAT TO DO WHEN YOU FALL OFF THE BANDWAGON

Let's be clear. You're going to fall off the metaphorical bandwagon at times when pursuing your goals. Expect that it's going to happen. Setting and achieving big goals is not an easy task. If you set an unrealistic and perfectionistic standard that you will never fall off the bandwagon or that if you do you're a failure, then your self-confidence and belief in your ability to reach your goals are almost guaranteed to wither.

Get the idea that you will never fail or have off days out of your head now. I'll say it again. You ***will fall off the bandwagon***! What differentiates those who continue to be successful after falling off and those who don't is how they handle this.

If you look at falling off the bandwagon in black-and-white terms, you'll see it as a personal failure, and will want to throw in the towel. But if you see it as a learning opportunity, then you will actually improve and grow. This

---

[55] Gollwitzer & Sheeran (2006). Implementation intentions and goal achievement: A meta-analysis of effects and processes. Advances in Experimental Social Psychology, 38, 69-119.

is part of the Growth Mindset I mentioned earlier in this book. Recall that having a Growth Mindset refers to the belief that you can improve with hard work. You need to adopt an attitude that embraces these setbacks. Even using the term "failure" is not at all accurate.

One thing you need to understand is that our brains accept our thoughts as truths if left unchecked. This fact is the core of the most successful forms of psychological treatment, including Cognitive-Behavioral Therapy and Acceptance and Commitment Therapy. These therapies focus on dealing with our thoughts and interpretations of events.

If you interpret your setback and label it as a "failure," then it's more likely to lead to further failure. If you embrace these events as learning experiences that can help you become better, then you'll come out of it even closer to your goals. The best basketball player to ever play in the NBA knew this all too well and credits it to his success. Michael Jordan said:

"I've missed more than 9,000 shots in my career. I've lost almost 300 games. 26 times, I've been trusted to take the game-winning shot and missed. I've failed over and over and over again in my life. And that is why I succeed."

So embrace setbacks as opportunities for learning. To do anything else is a guarantee that you won't achieve your full potential.

Procrastination and the Myth of Inspiration

Have you ever found that you set a goal for yourself but start to peter out after a few days or weeks? Maybe you decided that you were going to be getting up 30 minutes earlier to do cardio or work on that book you've finally decided to write. You start out with good intentions. You start out strong. Then you procrastinate. You know it's important to you and you're not sure what went wrong. You wonder how you're going to reach your potential if you can't keep on track and be constantly motivated.

Well, you're not alone. The truth is, we all struggle with this. Earlier in my life, I struggled with sticking to my goals. In high school, I knew I should have been trying to get good grades by consistently studying, but I couldn't get myself to follow through on these goals. It almost ruined my life.

Setting a goal is usually the easy part. But the idea that you can stay motivated by relying on the inspiration that motivated you to set the goal in the first place is flawed. It's not in line with what we know about the brain.

Something you find inspiring can only be inspiring for so long. Your brain simply can't stay in a hyped-up inspired state for long. It's designed to return to a state of equilibrium or balance. Some of you may recall this from grade 10 biology. It's called homeostasis. Your brain habituates to it. It's really not much different than what happens when you consume caffeine every day. Your brain just gets used to it and you develop tolerance which reduces the effect the caffeine has beyond a normal state.

That's why inspirational speeches can be highly motivating in the short-term, but usually don't lead to lasting change. Motivational speakers are highly sought after because they can bring up powerful emotions in the moment. When we feel strong emotions, we feel moved and inspired to act.

But strong emotions don't last. Our brains won't let them. Strong emotions also prevent us from thinking clearly, from grasping what it will actually take or what will need to be given up to achieve your goals. This is why relying on inspiration alone doesn't lead to lasting progress.

Let me tell you a little secret that is backed by tons of scientific research. Real progress on big goals doesn't happen because of a number of moments of inspiration. It happens because of hard and persistent work, day-in and day-out, regardless of your level of inspiration and motivation. It's not as sexy as what you see in the movies.

Get the idea that you need to feel inspired or motivated to work on your goals out of your head. If you allow it to stay there, you'll never achieve your goals or reach your full potential. American artist Chuck Close had it right when he said "Inspiration is for amateurs. The rest of us just show up and get to work."

The real secret to staying motivated and reaching your goals is to work on your goals *no matter what you feel like doing*. It doesn't matter if you feel energized or inspired to get up early and hit the gym or work on your book. Just do it. You may find yourself saying "I'm too tired" or "I'm not feeling it today." Just do it.

The most important differentiator found in those who achieve their goals and accomplish great things is that they don't live their lives dictated by their immediate feelings, urges, level of inspiration, energy, mood, or immediate circumstances. They don't let these states or circumstances dictate their actions. Instead, they decide what to do based on their deepest values, purpose, and goals and then do the work regardless. If you understand and implement this one principle into your life, you'll make real progress.

Why 'Listening to Your Gut' Is Sometimes Bad Advice

As highlighted throughout this book, successful people know themselves well, recognize their strengths and weaknesses, and then live their lives based on their deepest values, beliefs, mission, purpose, and goals — not based on their immediate urges, moods, or circumstances.

It's easy to get sidetracked or fall into the trap of waiting to take action on something until you're in the mood or the time feels right. Some people call this procrastination. If we base our decisions solely on our moods and energy levels, we will rarely get anything done. Lots of people are creative when they feel like it, but you're only going to become successful if you do it when you don't feel like it. After all, we're talking about achieving your important goals, not a hobby.

One of the reasons we have a hard time doing things we know we should be doing, or stopping ourselves from doing things we know we shouldn't be doing, is the result of thousands of years of evolution. The reality is our brains are biased to find fault, see danger, and predict pain when there may be nothing there. These are often experienced as "gut reactions."

These were really helpful when we were roaming the Savannah, as there were potential dangers everywhere and we had to avoid them if we wanted to survive. This helped us err on the side of caution. These biases are often called Cognitive Distortions because they are distorted ways of seeing the world.

These patterns of thinking are still hard-wired in our brains today. When we don't feel overly inspired to work on our goals, our brains often fall back on cognitive distortions. Two common ones are fortune-telling and catastrophizing.

When we don't want to start a task, we often fall into fortune-telling, with our brain tending to automatically predict a negative outcome such as not being able to do a good job. Of course, there is usually little evidence to support the prediction, which is why it is referred to as a distortion.

Catastrophizing refers to our brain's tendency to take it a step further and predict a horrible outcome despite little evidence to support this. Catastrophizing can also take the form of predicting that a task will be unbearable when, at worst, it may be only mildly uncomfortable. So remember that these are automatic biases our brains fall back on that are often wrong. Always taking your "gut reaction" or that little doubting voice in your head seriously is going to prevent you from achieving your goals.

KNOW YOUR GUT'S BIASES

Knowing your Basic Personality Tendencies will help you predict when you are likely to activate these cognitive distortions. Here are some examples of when fortune-telling and catastrophizing may be triggered depending on your unique personality profile:

- **Average-to-High on Negative Emotions:** In situations where you may experience stress such as when you're going into a big competition like the Olympic trials or playoffs, or face a work deadline. You may feel paralyzed to take action due to your brain's tendency to try to convince you that you will crumble under the pressure.

- **Average-to-Low on Extraversion:** In situations where you will be facing a lot of stimulation, especially social stimulation like your work or team's Christmas party. You may end up deciding not to go or experience undue stress beforehand due to distorted thinking.

- **Average-to-High on Extraversion:** When you'll be facing a lot of down time or under-stimulation. Your brain may predict that having to study plays for your upcoming game or working on a proposal will be unbearably boring. The reality is that it may be somewhat boring, but not unbearable.

- **Average-to-Low on Openness:** In situations where you will be exposed to new and non-traditional activities, new ideas, or new ideologies. For example, your biases may come up when you're "forced" to spend significant amounts of time with people with different religious or political perspectives.

- **Average-to-Low on Motivation:** When you have to get yourself to do things you know you should be doing, but don't want to do, like working out.

- **Average-to-Low on Agreeableness:** In situations where you are expected to open up to others or follow another leader who you're not sold on. This can be when a new coach or manager who you've heard negative things about comes on board, or if you're asked to attend a "team-building" retreat with co-workers that you're only lukewarm about.

As you can imagine, there are many other examples of how your Basic Personality Tendencies will interact with your situation to trigger cognitive distortions. See if you can come up with some examples of your own.

Knowing your personality will help you become more aware of when your brain will be more likely to activate these biases. This awareness will arm you with a skeptical attitude toward your predictions, immediate reactions or "gut feelings" in these situations.

THE 5-MINUTE RULE

The most effective strategy to overcome a perceived lack of motivation and our cognitive distortions is what is called The 5-Minute Rule and it's backed by science.[56] The 5-Minute Rule is simple. When you don't feel like doing something you know you should do, such as getting up and hitting the gym, start working on a project, or doing your weekly planning, you make a deal with yourself. You agree to do the activity for five minutes and *then* decide whether you want to do it or not.

The only way to test the idea of whether you really want to be doing something is to do it for five minutes. After five minutes you can decide to stop. You have to be serious and give yourself full permission to stop. If it turns out to be as bad as you predicted, or worse, give yourself permission to stop.

The reality is, 95 out of 100 times you'll find that your predictions were wrong and you can keep going. If you do this one activity from this chapter on a regular basis, I guarantee you will be much more likely to reach your goals and will be ahead of about 95 percent of your competition.

WHAT TO DO WHEN PLAGUED BY SELF-DOUBT

If you do all the things noted above and in previous chapters, problems with motivational struggles will essentially be a thing of the past. But some days everything just seems like an uphill battle even when you do get yourself started. This is often because you get hooked by your self-doubt.

---

[56] Foreman & Pollard (2011). Introducing Cognitive Behavioural Therapy (CBT): A Practical Guide.

The first thing to remember is that self-doubt is normal. You're always going to have at least some self-doubt. Why? Because that's what our brains were designed to do. And the reality is having self-doubt is a good thing because it motivates you to avoid danger and to improve as I noted in Chapter 13.

Imagine you're preparing for the biggest competition in your life. Maybe it's the Olympics, or maybe you're about to pitch your startup idea on Shark Tank. Do you think it would be better if, in the weeks and months leading up to these events, you had zero self-doubt?

You may want to answer yes, but the real answer is no. Having no doubts can lead you to underestimate your competition or how hard something is going to be. As noted in Chapter 12, this can make you complacent and unmotivated.

So, self-doubt is your friend. You can't eliminate it. You need to capitalize on what it offers you. It pushes you to be better.

Sometimes, despite the knowledge that self-doubt is normal and can be helpful, we can't seem to shake it. When this happens, try the strategies below.

Keep in mind that the following strategies only work when used sparingly. As noted earlier, the brain always wants to stay in a state of homeostasis. So your brain will habituate to these strategies pretty quickly. If you try to use these every day, or even every other day, they will quickly lose their effectiveness.

- **Ask yourself some powerful questions.** Simply asking yourself the following questions can often get you out of your funk. Think about the goal you are trying to achieve. Then ask yourself:

  - Why is this goal important to me?

  - What will happen if I achieve my goal? How will my life be different?

- What will happen, or what's at stake, if I don't achieve my goal?

When we're in a bad mood or feel unmotivated, we often have a particular set of neural networks in our brains that are activated. These act as a negative filter or lens and are related to cognitive distortions described earlier. These networks bias your mind toward seeing the negative in yourself, the world around you, and your past and future.

If you are average-to-high on Negative Emotions, then you will be more prone to falling into these states. When these networks are activated, it's almost impossible to spontaneously think in a more realistic, positive, and optimistic way. The following exercise will force your mind to reactivate the neural networks that are active when you're feeling positive, hopeful, optimistic, competent, and triumphant.

- **Relive past successes and peak experiences.** To do this, make sure you have about 5 to 10 minutes without interruption:

  - Turn off all alerts from your computer, phone, and gadgets. Put a Do Not Disturb sign on your door. Do whatever you have to do to make sure you can put all of your attention into this.

  - Sit and close your eyes.

  - Take six slow and long breaths over one minute. Do this by breathing in slowly through your nose to the count of five seconds. Then without pausing, slowly breathe out through your mouth for another five seconds. This will increase your heart rate variability which leads to a relaxed but focused state that can bring cognitive clarity. More on this in the upcoming books in this series.

  - Now, think back to a time when you achieved something that was meaningful to you, or a time when you had a peak experience in your life. It should be a time when you were performing near your potential, when you felt alive, absorbed in what you were doing, and excited. It helps when this was a challenging experience in which you ended up triumphing.

- Imagine and relive how you worked hard to overcome the challenges. Do not skip this step. You need to recall how you went through tough times and came out on top.

As an example, one of my peak experiences was the successful defense of my Ph.D. dissertation. It was years in the making and I pulled out all the strategies I could think of to get myself prepared. I was filled with a combination of self-doubt ("what if I fail?") and excitement ("if I pass this, I will finally have my Ph.D.!"). It started out worse than I thought when I fielded some really tough questions and critiques and realized that some of the committee members were playing hardball! But I eventually settled in and got my bearings. I got in the zone and got on a roll. By the end of it, I felt I could do another three hours. I felt great and got lots of positive feedback from some of the audience members and the committee. I felt on top of the world. In my mind I recalled how I was at the bottom of my class in junior high and most of high school and how far I had come.

This achievement felt so good because I not only beat the odds, what others thought I was capable of and my original self-doubts in my academic abilities, I did it all because I followed my passions. Your peak experience may be much different than mine. What matters is that it's something that you're proud of and where you performed well. Don't be humble!

- Now, in your mind, relive your peak experience as if it were happening again for the first time. Imagine it happening through your own eyes, in the first person. Use all of your senses. Vividly imagine what you saw, heard, felt, and even smelled if you can recall. Even if you can't recall all the details, feel free to elaborate somewhat. If it's easier for you, describe it out loud or write it out. Whatever works for you is fine.

- Stay in the moment for at least 3 to 5 minutes. Don't judge what you're doing. Just be there again. Really focus on the positive feelings you had when you were peaking or when it was over. Bask in it as long as you want.

Next, you can either get to work or move on to the next exercises.

- Envision yourself successfully achieving one of your goals, whether it be a longer-term goal or simply the goal for the day. To do this, follow the same lead-in process as above — get privacy, close your eyes, breathe six slow and long breaths over one minute. Then imagine yourself in detail overcoming any challenges and succeeding at your goal by incorporating as many senses as possible. Again, it's essential for you to imagine all the potential challenges you could face and how you will overcome them. Do this for 1 to 5 minutes.

- Call a trusted friend or relative. Sometimes when we are so stuck in a rut of low motivation or self-doubt, we need to hear some inspirational words from someone we care about.

  - Tell them about the difficulty you're having. It may be feeling unmotivated, fearful, or self-doubting.

  - Tell them you have a negative filter activated and are having a hard time seeing things optimistically, realistically, and positively.

  - Ask them if they would be willing to help you remember previous successes, how far you've come, what you have to offer the world, and if true, how proud they are of you.

- Look back at your goals and progress. This can serve to remind you how far you've come and how you've overcome a lot of resistance before today.

- If all else fails, decide that maybe today is not going to be as productive as you had hoped — and accept this. We all need down time to perform at our best. Sometimes high achievers develop unrealistically perfectionistic ideas that they should be working on their big goals all the time. The mind and body often can't keep up with this pace. If you try, you're going to burn out and underperform in the long run. Taking time off is important. Athletes definitely need rest days for their bodies to recover, but also for their minds to rebound. For those of you whose work is creative, a day or two away from it almost always results in new ideas and a refreshed perspective. Rest, distraction, and daydreaming are essential for creativity as well. So listen to your mind and body!

Know What to Focus On When

As noted in the last chapter, there is process focus and outcome focus just as there are process and outcome goals. Most of the time, we want to have a process focus when working on a task.

When you have a process focus, you are in the present moment focusing fully on the task at hand. This is critical for peak performance. You see, our brains have limited resources. To perform at our best at whatever task we're doing, whether we are an entrepreneur pitching a big idea to key investors or an NHL goalie trying to stop a puck in an overtime shootout, we will perform better if we are fully focused on the task at hand in the *present moment*. And when I say the present moment, I don't mean plus or minus 10 minutes. I mean right now. When our attention or focus shifts to what happened even a minute ago, or what may happen in the next minute, we are diverting precious brain power away from where it should be focused.

So imagine this: You're a goalie in a shootout and 30 seconds ago you let the last shot in. The next player is barreling down the ice to try to score on you. If you're still thinking about what you did wrong on the last shot, or what it will mean for your team's playoff chances if you lose the shootout, a big chunk of your brain is not attending to the task at hand, and you're guaranteed to underperform. You might as well put beer in your water bottle or tie one hand behind your back because a mind that isn't fully focused on the immediate moment is an impaired mind.

Same goes if you're pitching your complex idea to investors and you're thinking about why the guy in the blue shirt just got up and walked out of the room. Your pitch will suffer.

Process focus is similar to what is commonly referred to as mindfulness. Mindfulness generally refers to being fully present in the moment. As you can imagine, having a process focus and being mindful can also be helpful in many other aspects of your life. Just imagine trying to have a meaningful conversation with your significant other if your mind is focused on things like what you're going to watch on Apple TV later tonight!

When we are in the zone or flow, our focus is on the process, not the outcome. Many of the strategies outlined in this book and the upcoming books in this series will enable you to more easily get into the zone or in flow.

Recall that having an outcome focus occurs when you are focused on the result or what you want to achieve. There are times when you want to have an outcome focus, such as when your task is relatively simple and possibly boring and you notice your motivation or energy is low. Bringing to mind your outcome goals, or focusing on what you're hoping your current activity will achieve, can keep you moving forward.

So when you're about to get on the ice for the beginning of the shootout and you feel exhausted and unmotivated, that's the perfect time to focus on what it will mean if your team wins. Or if it's late the night before your big pitch to investors and you're tired and want to check in for the night, but still have important work to do, you may want to remind yourself of how landing these investors could catapult your start-up to a level you only dreamed of. This will help boost your motivation and energy.

Let me give you a real example. Jay was a top-level mixed martial artist who contacted me hoping to take his game up a notch. He actually was doing really well, but was smart enough to know he wanted to leave no stone unturned when it came to his mental game. One thing he didn't realize was that he was focusing on process and outcome at the wrong times, based on bad advice from a former coach.

During cardio training with the heavy bag, Jay's former coach would repeatedly tell him to focus on his form and the sound of the bag when he hit it. In other words, during a boring task that was meant to build up endurance, his coach was telling him to focus on the process. Jay found these cardio drills boring and exhausting and found himself giving up early as a result.

Also, when Jay was about to step into the ring, his former coach would encourage him to imagine what it will mean to win. But Jay was both high on Negative Emotions and Motivation, so he didn't need any help getting emotionally activated or motivated. Thinking of the outcome of winning and what it would mean only made him go from activated to over-activated and nervous. During the matches, his former coach would repeatedly yell from his corner "win this one and you're in the UFC!" So in the middle of the match, Jay would be thinking of what it would be like to achieve his dream of competing in the UFC. As you can imagine, this strategy only served to make him over-activated and used up his brain's precious attentional resources.

Once I explained to Jay the difference between process and outcome focus, it immediately made intuitive sense to him. He also relayed this to his new coaches. We worked on using an outcome focus when he was doing mindless cardio drills, or when he had to motivate himself to hit the gym when he was tired.

So now when he does mindless cardio drills, instead of focusing on the sounds of the bag or his form, he focuses on what it would mean to achieve his dream of a UFC contract.

Similarly, just before and during competition, Jay now focuses on the process, or exactly what he has to do. He strives to stay in the present moment. With the aid of his new coaches, he learned to stay 100 percent focused on his opponent and look for openings. Just these two simple changes in his focus improved his motivation and energy during training, and his ability to read and react during the fight.

There are a number of other strategies to improve your ability to focus that are too numerous to include in this book. These include attention training, meditation, neurofeedback, cue-words, and others. These will be further elaborated on in the upcoming books in this series.

FIND YOUR ENERGY 'SWEET SPOT'

Best-selling author, biohacker, and angel investor Tim Ferriss does his best writing late in the evenings. In fact, he does his best writing between 10 p.m. and 5 a.m.!

Kurt Vonnegut did his best work between about 6 a.m. and 10 a.m. Still others like Charles Dickens did their best work from 9 a.m. to around 3:00 p.m.

And still others like Mozart worked in spurts throughout the day, but generally did no creative work during regular working hours.

As much as we'd all like to have unlimited energy and cognitive powers like Eddie Morra in *Limitless*, there is no super drug like the fictional NZT (and believe me, I've researched and tried just about everything out there).

For now, we need to understand that we have energy cycles. Just as there are sleep cycles for stages of sleep that last 70 to 90 minutes, there are similar rhythms that dictate how alert and energized we feel when we're awake.

These 24-hour cycles are referred to as the ultradian rhythms. We don't stay equally energized and alert throughout the day.[57]

Research suggests it is best to take breaks from work every hour to hour-and-a-half. Ideally, during your breaks you should engage in more mindless or less cognitively demanding tasks.[58]

When you are engaging in cognitively demanding tasks, your brain is mostly producing a lot of fast waves when measured on an EEG. These fast waves represent high levels of cortical activity and are called beta waves. When you're resting or engaging in less cognitively demanding activities, your brain goes into a slower state. When recovering between bouts of work, you want to get your brain into more of an alpha state, which is a slower, idling state.

Ideally, you would want to engage in some of the strategies outlined in the upcoming books in this series, such as Heart Rate Variability biofeedback, exercising, mindfulness meditation, or any other activity you can do mindfully such as walking, cleaning, sorting, etc. You can also get more tips from my website: FriesenPerformance.com

While not exactly the same as your energy cycles, some research has found correlations between two of the Basic Personality Tendencies and whether you are more of a morning or a night person. Generally, morning-people tend to be higher on Motivation, whereas those who are night-owls tend to be higher on Negative Emotions.[59] Of course, there are many exceptions to this.

The bottom line: It's important to know what times during the day you work best. Some of us do our best work in the morning, others in the afternoon, while others late in the evening. If you don't already know this

---

[57] For more detail on this, check out author Tony Schwartz's website: http://theenergyproject.com/

[58] See work by the Draugiem Group described here: https://goo.gl/1UUe1M
And Ariga et al. (2011). Brief and rare mental 'breaks' keep you focused: Deactivation and reactivation of task goals preempt vigilance decrements. Cognition, 118(3), 439-443.

[59] Tonetti et al. (2009). Relationship between circadian typology and Big Five personality domains. Chronobiology International, 26(2), 337-347.

about yourself, set up a little experiment where you try doing your work at different times of the day and see what works best.

Once you know what time of day you do your best work, plan your day accordingly. Definitely don't waste this precious commodity on tasks like email, meetings, or phone calls. If you do your best work in the mornings, then that is when you need to schedule work on your big, important goals.

For many, remembering to pull yourself away from what you're doing is the hardest part of staying on track. This is especially true for those high on the tendency of Motivation. I know this is the most difficult part for me. Once I get into something, it's really hard for me to disengage and work on something else if the first task isn't complete.

One solution is to set a timer on your computer or phone to go off in 60 to 90 minutes to remind you to stop what you're doing for about 5 to 15 minutes. I used this strategy when studying at university while trying to learn content for exams and it paid off.

HOW TO TAME THE BEAST OF TECHNOLOGY

In today's modern world, we are constantly hyper-connected with our smartphones, tablets, computers, or smartwatches. These technologies have led to tremendous progress, but they're not without their downsides.

Don't get me wrong here. I'm no Luddite. But reaching our potential means going against the grain. To be successful, you have to not only battle yourself, but also the external world's pressure to stay with the status quo. Without plans and strategies, you will be victim to the wind, getting blown every which way. You need to seize the rudder and steer yourself in the direction *you want*, not what society wants from you. Not even what the lazy and self-protective part of you wants.

One example how modern technology gets in our way is by distracting us constantly. Our smartphones and computers are the biggest culprits. We are bombarded with texts, alerts, alarms, calls, emails, social media status updates and on and on. Not surprisingly, there are brain mechanisms that are at play here. Suffice it to say — you guessed it — our dopamine reward systems are in play again.

Every time you engage with your gadgets by doing things like checking email, texts, social media, and surfing the net, the dopamine reward pathway is activated in your brain. Dopamine's role in the brain is pretty complicated, but one of the things it controls is your motivation to seek out or search for things that are potentially rewarding or pleasurable. Note I used the word "potentially."

The more unpredictable getting a reward or experiencing some pleasure is, the more the dopamine system kicks in, which makes you want to keep searching and checking. And make no mistake, this mechanism in your brain is *very strong*. Turns out our text messages, emails, phone calls and social media posts arrive fairly randomly, which enhances your dopamine response even more!

Decades ago, psychologists discovered the best way to control both animal and human behavior was by using rewards. They found that the most effective timing and frequency of rewards was to use variable schedules of reinforcement. We now know that this is related to the dopamine response noted above. And guess what? Checking email, texts, social media, and surfing the web provide us with a variable schedule of reward reinforcement. So it's no wonder we can't get anything done!

If you're going to make any progress in athletics, art, business, or your profession, then you need to take back control of your life. You need to engage in what Cal Newport calls Deep Work — engaging in deep, distraction-free work.[60]

Even if you are not very high on the tendency of Motivation, you can take back control of your productivity. So how do you do it?

- The overall solution is to hack your brain and hack your environment. First of all, you need to schedule time to work on

---

[60] Newport (2016). Deep work: Rules for focused success in a distracted world: http://goo.gl/VHHHoH

your important goals. This has to be given the same priority level as something like a doctor's appointment. It's basically non-negotiable. When the time comes to work on that goal, you need to eliminate any possible distractions. So turn off your phone, email, social media, and even your Internet if possible. Without any beeps, buzzes, or alerts from your devices, the dopamine reward-seeking pathway in your brain will relax a little and let you get down to business. You should start using this strategy when you're doing any important work.

- Get to know the Settings tab on your devices. Stop all the email, social media, and other alerts from popping up. If you don't know how, check YouTube for instructions on how to do this on your specific device. This will prevent distractions and allow you to better focus on what really matters to you. In addition, on most smartphones, you can use the Do Not Disturb setting. Basically, it prevents your phone from ringing or alerting you about anything. If you're afraid you'll miss an emergency call, you can set your phone to alert you only when someone from your Favorites calls, or if someone calls twice in a row. You can also schedule your phone to go into Do Not Disturb mode at specific times each day when you know you're going to be focusing on important tasks.

- Another problem is email. Although it seems glaringly clear now, it took Tim Ferriss and his book *The 4-Hour Workweek* to point out the obvious. Set particular times during the day to check your email. He recommends we even put this schedule on our email signature or autoresponder, so others don't freak out when we don't instantly reply to their emails.

- The same idea can be used for checking social media. Allow yourself to only check at pre-planned intervals, either as breaks during the workday or after work. This takes willpower at first, but once you've made it a habit, it will become automatic and no longer require you to exert any willpower.

I'm not at all against email and social media. But use it to reward yourself after you've completed tasks. This one I learned from my mother. She'd get up early in the morning on weekends and complete all of her household chores like cleaning and vacuuming before she allowed herself to sit down and enjoy the rest of the day in leisurely activities, which for my mom mostly involved reading and more reading. Rewarding yourself after you've done work will serve to make you less distractible and also motivate you to engage in difficult tasks, since our brains are primarily motivated by rewards.

How to Let Go at the End of the Day

Many high achievers have a hard time disengaging and detaching from work when they get home or when it's time to relax. They also have a hard time acknowledging success.

Those of you who are on the higher side of Motivation will be most susceptible to these, due to your tendency to work long and hard and to place high standards on yourself. If you are also high on Negative Emotions, winding down and acknowledging what went well may also be hard for you. There are some simple strategies you can implement at the end of the workday to help with this:

- Write down or mentally review what you accomplished today. You want to do what I call the 3 Things Exercise. First write out or mentally review three things that you did well today. This could be as simple as remembering to take breaks every 90 minutes. For those of you who are average-to-high on Negative Emotions or Motivation, this part will be challenging. Your mind will have little difficulty picking out what you did wrong or didn't achieve. This exercise will help force your mind to see things realistically and acknowledge what went well. The more you do this, the easier it will become, as your more dormant realistic and optimistic neural networks will be getting a daily workout.

- Next, write out or mentally review three things that did not go so well. *But* you must then do the following. Reframe these in terms of what you learned from the experiences and provide yourself a set of instructions on how to improve upon them. So maybe you were training and got a stomach cramp after eating too close to practice. Instead of saying, "I learned to not eat too close to training", say "I will eat at least 180 minutes before training." Or better yet, use what we learned about If-Then planning by saying "If it is three hours before training, I will eat." As noted earlier, your mind responds well to specific instructions on *what to do,* and not so well in terms of *what not to do.* It's like a race-car driver. They are instructed to look where they want to go, not at the wall they are trying to avoid.

- For any unfinished tasks, write down exactly when and where you will finish them tomorrow or later in the week. You need to write down exactly where, when, and how you will do this. For example, "I will call the supplier back right after my lunch break tomorrow at 1 p.m." This will help you mentally let go of any lingering unfinished tasks that are taking up space in your working memory.

- Make a plan via a to-do list for tomorrow. The plan will take into consideration what you learned from the preceding steps, but also what your weekly goals are. This was also outlined earlier in this chapter.

- On your way home, get in touch with some of your values and goals that revolve around your family, health, hobbies, community, or other areas other than work. If driving, you can record yourself describing these goals and values so that you can listen to them. Or once you arrive home and turn off your car, take a few minutes to either mentally review these goals and values or read them. For the latter, you can have them written out in your smartphone's notes feature, or have it written out on paper you keep in your wallet or glove box for easy access.

Resources:

Willpower: Rediscovering the Greatest Human Strength by Baumeister, Ph.D. and Tierney: http://goo.gl/HMMEoL

The Willpower Instinct: How Self-Control Works, Why It Matters, and What You Can Do to Get More of It by Kelly McGonical, Ph.D.: http://goo.gl/CQ2l13

Deep Work: Rules for Focused Success in a Distracted World by Cal Newport, Ph.D.: http://goo.gl/VHHHoH

The 4-Hour Workweek by Tim Ferriss: http://goo.gl/gia0E5

CONCLUSION

The fact that you have arrived at this point in the book tells me that you are someone who wants to achieve big and meaningful goals in your life. You want to make sure you're doing everything in your power to make your dreams a reality.

You are now in possession of an effective step-by-step process to get you there that is derived from the three best sources of knowledge — science, experience, and results. So you can feel confident that following the steps in this book has brought you closer to your goals than ever before.

At the beginning of this book, I asked you to answer the questions below:

Have you:

- Felt different from others, but were not quite sure why?

- Felt unsure of your purpose in this life?

- Wondered whether you were focusing on the right goals in your life?

- Felt certain paths you took, or decisions you made, just didn't seem to fit?

- Wondered whether your chosen career path was right for you?

- Felt you were just going through the motions in your life?

- Had trouble staying motivated and focused on a big goal?

- Established your big goals, but couldn't seem to stay motivated long enough to make them a reality?

- Felt unsure of yourself and in your ability to accomplish your goals?

The information, strategies, and exercises in this book should help you gain some clarity and actionable strategies for any of the above questions you answered yes to as you begin this journey.

My main objective in writing this book is for you to have a logical step-by-step process for figuring out how to work effectively toward the dreams and goals that are right for you.

In this book, you learned that, to be successful, you need to adopt particular ways of seeing the world, including:

- Accepting yourself for who you are and working with or around what you are given. This includes knowing your personality, values, strengths, weaknesses, and passions.

- Living your life and setting goals congruent with your personality, values, strengths, passions, mission, and purpose, not based on your immediate urges, moods, or circumstances.

- Knowing that you have much more control over the trajectory of your life than you or others realize. At the same time, you know that even though you are steering your ship, you can only control yourself. You understand and accept that you can't control what the world throws in your path, but you can control how you react to these obstacles. You refuse to be a victim of life. You know that you can anticipate and act before the world acts upon you. You know that if you keep pushing forward you will eventually reach your destination.

- Accepting that you will repeatedly go through tough times. Tough times are par for the course for those who do big things. You know that's how the world works, and so there is no point fighting or complaining about it. Without difficult times and failures, there is no learning. You reframe setbacks as opportunities for growth. You know that nothing worth achieving comes without a struggle. You know there's a difference between suffering and struggling. As the Dalai Lama wrote: "Pain is inevitable. Suffering is optional." You now know that successful people struggle and feel pain, but don't suffer because they are living their lives and pursuing goals that are in line with who they are, what they value, and what they believe to be their purpose or mission. To them and to you, it is worth it.

So the question becomes, do you want to live with regrets because you didn't do all you could to achieve your dreams and goals?

Or do you want to be able to look yourself in the mirror each day and confidently say you are doing everything in your power to reach the right goals for you?

I believe that the fact that you read this book to the end means your answer is the latter.

By reading this book and applying what you learned, you have taken the first step to unleash your potential. There is no more need to settle for a life of living below your true potential. You are now armed with knowledge of who you are, what you really want, and how to make it happen. You now have a path to achieving great things with your life and I'm confident that you're going to make it happen!

At the same time, I hope you saw that the process is not necessarily easy or simple. I hope this book helped you realize that we only get one shot at this life and that you don't want regrets. You now know how to make sure you're focusing on and achieving the right goals for you. You're ready to tweak your mind, body, and brain to achieve and perform at the highest level.

Want more? Check out my website FriesenPerformance.com for information on how to take your game to the next level, including free information such as articles and podcast interviews, in addition to online programs, workshops, personal coaching/consulting, speaking engagements, and information on the release date for the second book in this series.

You can also join my mailing list at <u>FriesenPerformance.com</u> to stay up do date on ways to take your performance in sports, work, and life to the next level!